W9-BJS-577

NO EASY VICTORIES

VICTORIES

Black Americans and the Vote

CLARENCE LUSANE

NO EASY VICTORIES

VICTORIES

Black Americans and the Vote

CLARENCE LUSANE

THE AFRICAN-AMERICAN EXPERIENCE

FRANKLIN WATTS
A DIVISION OF GROLIER PUBLISHING
New York • London • Toronto • Sydney • Danbury, Connecticut

Photo credits ©: AP/Wide World Photos: pp. 62, 98 (both photos), 123; Jay Mallin: pp. 91, 96; Library of Congress: pp. 16, 85; New York Public Library, Schomburg Collection: p.14; New York Public Library, Special Collections: p. 45; UPI/Bettmann: pp. 10, 53, 56, 59, 61, 64, 67, 76, 78, 89, 104, 106, 129, 130; UPI/Corbis-Bettmann: p. 102.

Lusane, Clarence, 1953–
    No Easy Victories: Black Americans and the Vote/by Clarence Lusane.
    p. cm. — (The African-American Experience) Includes bibliographical references and index.
    ISBN 0-531-11270-5
    1. Afro-Americans—Politics and government. 2. Afro-American politi-cians—History. 3. Afro-Americans—Suffrage. I. Title. II. Series.
E185.L87 1996
323.1'196073—dc20   CIP
                                                      96-21469

CONTENTS

CHAPTER ONE
Blacks in Politics Before the Civil War   11

CHAPTER TWO
The Reconstruction Era   20

CHAPTER THREE
The All-Black Towns Movement   32

CHAPTER FOUR
The Fight for Black Political Power,
    1900-1965   41

CHAPTER FIVE
Black Members of Congress,
1928-1965   50

CHAPTER SIX
The 1965 Voting Rights Act   66

CHAPTER SEVEN
The Congressional Black Caucus   81

CHAPTER EIGHT
The 1980s and the Quest for the White House 100

CHAPTER NINE
Black Elected Officials in the 1990s   117

APPENDIX
Black Presidential Candidates   137

SOURCE NOTES   141

INDEX   154

Dedication

To my grandmother, the Hon. Carrie "Mudear" Sager, Chief Poll Inspector Muscoda Improvement Association in Bessemer, Jefferson County, Alabama, the first and only black elected official in our family, the only African American to hold that position, and the first African American in her district to win the right to vote by overcoming every racist voting restriction and obstacle placed in front of her.

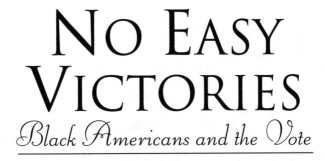

No Easy
Victories
Black Americans and the Vote

CLARENCE LUSANE

President Johnson signs the 1965 Voting Rights Act.

CHAPTER ONE

Blacks in Politics Before the Civil War

The small state of Vermont was the first to elect an African American to public office when Alexander Lucius Twilight won a seat in the state legislature in 1836.[1]

In September 1847, three thousand miles away, William A. Leisdesdorf won election to the San Francisco (then Yerba Buena) town council,[2] becoming the second black elected official in United States history.[3]

The area of Brownhelm, Ohio, was a haven for runaway slaves and home to a thriving abolitionist movement during the mid-1800s. On April 2, 1855, John Mercer Langston, a lawyer, became the nation's third known black elected official when he was elected township clerk on the ticket of the Liberty Party, one of the first major parties to nominate blacks for office.[4] Langston was perhaps the only black elected official who was in political office both before and after the Civil War.

Twilight's, Leisdesdorf's, and Langston's victories were the beginning of a long but little known history of the evolution of black electoral power that began with the birth of the new nation.

Prior to the Revolutionary War, there were no racial restrictions to voting in Maine, New Hampshire, Vermont, Massachusetts, Rhode Island, Maryland, and North Carolina, although free blacks could not hold office.[5] In these states, free blacks faced the same voting obstacles as most whites: lack of property and wealth. In addition to enslaved African Americans and American Indians, certain religious groups were prevented from voting as were women except in the states of New Jersey (1776–1876) and Massachusetts (1690–1780).[6]

Under the British monarchy, there were very few elected offices at all. England controlled the budding nation's economic, social, and political life, and resistance to that rule eventually led to the Revolution.

SLAVERY, THE FIGHT FOR INDEPENDENCE, AND BLACK POLITICAL RIGHTS

That a man of black and Indian heritage, a runaway slave, Crispus Attucks would be the first to give his life for independence was an irony that forced some to rethink their position on slavery and blacks' political rights.

Abigail Adams, a leader in the movement for women's rights and wife of John Adams, later the nation's second president, wrote in a 1774 letter to her husband that it was hypocritical and dishonest for whites to be fighting for freedom and not recognize that slaves "have as good a right to freedom as we have."[7]

When the people of the colonies declared their independence, they also had the opportunity to take a moral stand against slavery. The colonists' demands for liberty and individual freedom was clearly in contradiction with the enslavement of blacks. Too glaring to be ignored, slavery was condemned by a number of the revolutionary leaders in the harshest terms.

In a passage written for the Declararion of Independence by Thomas Jefferson that was not included in the final version, King George was severely criticized for promoting slavery.[8] This passage vanished from the Declaration as southern leaders of the revolution protested. Jefferson, George Washington, Patrick Henry, and others spoke out on occasion against slavery but were compromised by being slave owners themselves. During their public life, none of these men freed their slaves.

In order for northern leaders to win the southern states over to the notion of a federal union, the issues of slavery and full citizenship and political rights for blacks in the new nation were largely compromised or evaded. As much as possible, the delegates to the Constitutional Convention in Philadelphia in 1887 attempted to hide the shame of slavery. Although the issue was the one most fiercely fought at the convention, nowhere in the Constitution are the terms "slavery" or "slave" used.

At least one delegate to the Philadelphia convention was repulsed by the failure of the convention to end slavery. The ironically-named Luther Martin, a delegate from Maryland, stated that slavery was "inconsistent with the principles of the Revolution, and dishonorable to the American character to have such a feature in the Constitution."[9] Martin walked out of the convention in anger and fought against the ratification of the Constitution. He later traveled to a number of states and presented stinging condemnations of the Constitution in a futile effort to prevent its passage as long as it condoned slavery. In his address to the Maryland legislature, Martin criticized the passage extending the slave trade by stating, "The design of this clause is to prevent the General Government from prohibiting the importation of slaves: but the same reasons [that] caused them to strike out the word 'national' and not admit the word 'stamps,' influ-

Richard Allen established the African Methodist Episcopal Zion (AME) Church.

enced them here to guard against the word 'slaves.' They anxiously sought to avoid the admission of the expressions [that] might be odius in the ears of Americans, although they were willing to admit into their system those things [that] the expressions signified."[10] However, moral stands such as the one taken by Martin were rare and, in the end, had little impact on the ratification of the document.

For a time, laws existed that allowed free blacks to vote in both the North and even in the South. In 1780, nine of the thirteen existing states allowed free blacks to vote although with varying restrictions and qualifications.[11] Little documentation exists beyond these bare facts.

This small respite would not last, however. Soon after the new nation was consolidated, a steady decline in the political rights of free blacks began to occur. In 1802, President Thomas Jefferson disenfranchised free blacks in Washington, D.C. Jefferson's action was soon followed by Maryland in 1810, Tennessee in 1834, North Carolina in 1835, Pennsylvania in 1838, and Indiana in 1851. Every state that was admitted into the Union with the exception of Maine, restricted the vote to white males. At the time of the Civil War, free blacks could vote only in New York, New Hampshire, Vermont, Massachusetts, Rhode Island, and Maine,[12] and often under severe restrictions. In New York, for example, blacks were required to establish a three-year residency and to own property worth at least 250 dollars—a qualification that even most whites could not meet.

EARLY BLACK NATIONALISM AND THE U.S. POLITICAL SYSTEM

For some blacks, participation in the U.S. political system was not desirable. Black nationalism advocated unity within the black community, pride in Africa and its history and cultures, and armed uprising by the slaves. Many of the earliest nationalist leaders rejected efforts to change the political system so that blacks could participate more equally. Among those in the period before the Civil War were Richard Allen, Paul Cuffee, Prince Hall, Martin Delaney, Henry H. Garnet, Alexander Crummell, Edward Blyden, and Bishop Henry McNeal Turner.

Dr. Martin Delaney, Father of Black Nationalism

Black religious nationalism was born when Richard Allen was rebuffed in his efforts to integrate the Methodist Church. When he set up a storefront to minister to blacks, he was told by the Methodist Church to either give it up or be purged. He refused and was kicked out of the church. He formed the Free African Society and established the Bethel African Methodist Episcopal

Zion (AME) church in Philadelphia. In 1816, the AME was formally founded.

Most of the nationalists supported the idea of blacks going back to Africa. Near the beginning of the last century, Paul Cuffee, a former sea captain, founded the African Institute and was involved in taking 38 African Americans to newly-formed Sierre Leone. Toward the middle of the 1800s, journalist and physician Martin Delaney, known as the father of black nationalism, became the leading advocate of the Back-to-Africa movement. Delaney argued that blacks could never achieve equality in the United States and should migrate to Liberia. Delaney would also become one of the earliest black elected officals. In his remarkable career, he was one of only seventy-five black officers in the entire Union army.

After Delaney's death in 1885, Bishop Henry McNeal Turner became the leading spokesperson for black emigration. Turner formed the African Emigration Association, which later became the International Emigration Association, to facilitate the transportation of blacks to Africa. He supported blacks going to Liberia and called for reparations. Other leading repatriation activists included Alexander Crummell, a minister, active in the American Colonialization Society, and Edward Blyden, who emigrated to Liberia from the West Indies after first visiting the United States, and who became a strong advocate of African American migration to Africa.

PRE–CIVIL WAR POLITICAL PARTICIPATION BY BLACKS

The National Negro Convention Movement

In 1830, fifteen representatives—ministers, ex-slaves, business leaders, and newspapers editors—from five states gathered in Philadelphia and founded the National Negro Convention movement (NNC). It met six more times between 1831 and 1836, three times in the 1840s, and twice in the 1850s. It met for the last time in 1860, and changed its name to the National Equal Rights League. At its 1853 gathering, a resolution was passed that demanded for blacks the "complete and unrestricted right of suffrage, opening of admission to all colleges and universities, equal justice for all under the law, and repeal of America's racist laws."[13]

At many local meetings of the Negro Convention movement, issues of voting rights and putting pressure on elected officials dominated much of the discussion. The movement eventually split over which was the most effective strategy for African Americans: to remain in the United States and struggle for reform, or go to Canada and set up a colony of black American emigrants.

Blacks gave little support to the Democratic Party due to its pro-slavery party stance. Prior to the 1850s, free blacks gave their support to either the Federalist Party or the Whig Party, both of which opposed slavery. The Whig Party was, in the main, conservative and pro-business, but had been critical of slavery. In the 1850s, northern Whigs and southern Whigs split over a number of issues, including slavery, and the party soon died. Many of the northern Whigs would find a home in the newly-established Republican Party.

The Republican Party began in 1854 and was explicitly antislavery although for drastically different reasons than those of the abolitionists. While the abolitionists viewed slavery as wrong on moral grounds, the Republicans supported industrial growth of the United States and opposed the slave system as economically backward. Northern capitalists also recognized that to control the economy, they had to control the political structures. The ascension of Abraham Lincoln to the presidency in 1860 was a signal to Democrats and their southern followers that a new era was dawning. The conflict between the northern industrialists and midwestern farmers, on the one hand, and the southern slaveholders, on the other, would ultimately be resolved by the Civil War. Not only was the economic future of the country at stake, but also its political future.

Black activists and voters turned rapidly to the Republican Party. Frederick Douglass and others welcomed the Republican call for the end of slavery and the beginning of black suffrage. The March 1857 Dred Scott decision by the U.S. Supreme Court, which stated that blacks had no citizenship rights and that escaped slaves could be returned to their masters, also helped to push many blacks into the Republican camp. In the Scott case, Chief Justice Roger B. Taney wrote that blacks "had no rights which the white man was bound to respect."[14] The failed but frightening effort by John Brown to seize the Harper Ferry armory to launch a military fight to free the slaves also pushed the conflict over slavery to the breaking point. It would take the Civil War to resolve the issue of slavery. In order for the nation to go forward, the institution of slavery had to be ended.[15]

CHAPTER TWO

The Reconstruction Era

Jubilation was everywhere. Each day was an awakening to freedom's blessings.[1] By the tens of thousands, blacks stormed the political stage in the transforming years from 1867 to 1877, known as Radical Reconstruction. At the federal, state, and local levels, about two thousand black officals were elected for the period 1860–1877,[2] although participation was highest during the period 1867–1877. Blacks registered, voted, attended state constitutional conventions, and ran for office in overwhelming numbers. Black laborers and carpenters, ministers and teachers, campaigned for elected office. Election day was, for the new black voters, the most important day of the year. In the weeks leading to election day, blacks by the thousands gathered in meetings, parades, picnics, and strategy sessions to collectively fashion a line of march to victory.

At the same time, the period was one of the most difficult for African Americans. The majority of ex-slaves were unskilled, uneducated, and without resources. Black leaders were divided over what strategy would best suit the interests of the newly free slaves. Some advocated a return to Africa; others emigration to Canada or at least out of the south.

The entire southern region was suffering from the economic and social instability caused by the Civil War and the harsh penalties imposed by the victorious Lincoln government. Poor whites found themselves disenfranchised, propertyless, and in a similar economic state as that of blacks. However, rather than find unity with blacks against a common enemy, poor whites formed and joined new underground white supremacist organizations whose main purpose was to terrorize the black community. Groups such as the Ku Klux Klan, the Knights of the White Camelia, the White Brotherhood, Red Shirts, Pale Faces, and '76 Association emerged in the wake of the freedom of blacks. The KKK was formed in Pulaski, Tennessee, in 1866 by six former Confederate soldiers and made up initially of mostly poor whites who found efforts at black equality threatening.[3] Black politicians and activists were favorite targets of the KKK and the other groups.

Among the blacks who actually won political office during Reconstruction, there were 237 ministers, 125 carpenters, 50 barbers, 47 blacksmiths, 37 masons, 37 shoemakers, 172 teachers, 83 editors and publishers, 104 businessmen, 294 farmers, and 115 laborers. There were thousands more who ran and lost in nearly every jurisdiction in the South as well as a few outside of the region.[4]

Aware of their inexperience, blacks wanted nevertheless to participate in the political process. Former slave William Beverly Nash, who had been elected to the South Carolina Constitutional Convention and would later be appointed magistrate, reflected this willingness to overcome the past:

I believe, my friends and fellow-citizens, we are not prepared for this suffrage. But we can learn. Give a man tools and let him commence to use them, and in time he will learn the trade. So it is with voting. We may not understand it at the start, but in time we shall learn to do our duty.[5]

Although black women, like all women, could not vote, they were often on the front line defending the right of black males to vote or making sure that black males did not shirk from their voting responsibility. One white who opposed black suffrage was heard to complain, "The women are the head and fount of the opposition, some going to the polls to see the men voted right, threatening them with assassination if they did not vote as they wished."[6]

Some black politicians were weathy or became wealthy in office while others would die in poverty. One of the saddest cases was that of former Congressman Alonzo Jacob Ransier (1873–1874). Falling into poverty after leaving Congress, Ransier was forced eventually to take a job as a night watchman at the Custom House in Charleston, South Carolina. He ended up as a municipal street sweeper before his death at the early age of forty-eight.[7]

Virtually overnight, black voters became a force to deal with. In 1868, in the first presidential election following the Civil War and the Emancipation Proclamation, Republican candidate Ulysses S. Grant lost the majority of the white vote; however, he received virtually all of the nearly 500,000 black votes cast. This mobilized black vote contributed significantly to the passage of the Fifteenth Amendment on February 26, 1869, shortly after Grant took office.[8]

Blacks outnumbered whites in a number of southern states and held majorities of as much as ten-to-one in some black belt counties in the South.[9] These numbers translated into high registration rates. Black men were the majority of registered voters in five states: South Carolina, Mississippi, Alabama, Florida, and Louisiana;[10] 700,000 were black.[11] This leap in black power led one former Civil War veteran, General Sterling Price, to fret, "I pray to God that my fears for the future of the South may never be realized, but when the right is given the Negro to bring suit, testify before the courts, and vote in elections, you all had better be in Mexico."[12]

In an effort to protect their enfranchisement, blacks (and some whites) organized Loyal Leagues. The purpose of the leagues was "to secure the complete ascendancy of the true principles of popular government—equal liberty, education, and the elevation of the working men of the Nation, and the security of all by means of the elective franchise."[13] The leagues would later come under severe attack and many of its leaders were beaten and killed by the Ku Klux Klan and other white groups.

In order to be readmitted into the union, the Confederate states had to hold biracial conventions where new constitutions were to be written that pledge alligance to the federal government.[14] The conventions held in 1867 and 1868 varied in length from a brief twenty-three days in Alabama to almost four months in Mississippi. The newly emancipated and the highly educated blacks worked side by side with whites to draft constitutions that would be some of the most democratic documents produced up until that time. A significant percent of ex-slaves were involved in the conventions. In South Carolina (which began its historic convention on Tuesday, January 14, 1868) fifty-seven of the seventy-six blacks who participated in the convention, seventy-five percent, were former slaves. In Alabama, sixteen of eighteen blacks, 89 percent, were previously held in bondage.[15] Several highly educated blacks were involved in the deliberations. In South Carolina, there was Francis Louis Cardozo and Robert Brown Elliott. Cardozo had been educated at the

University of Glasgow while Elliott had matriculated at Eton. In Florida, Jonathan C. Gibbs had received degrees from Dartmouth and the Princeton Theological Seminary.[16] Additionally, there were a large number of educated and professional black leaders, including preachers, doctors, artists, lawyers, architects, and teachers, who returned from Canada to participate in the new southern society.[17]

White southerners derided the conventions without mercy. In Virginia, its convention was referred to as a "Convention of Kangaroos." In Louisiana, the event was termed, reflecting a local point of view, the "Congo Convention." In North Carolina, the so-called "Bones and Banjo Convention" was ridiculed in the press daily and, in Alabama, the meetings were generically called the "Black Crook Conventions."[18]

Undeterred and unafraid, blacks supported the conventions and turned out in large numbers to vote for the constitutions that the conventions created. In the 1869 vote for the state constitution in South Carolina, for instance, 69,000 of the 81,000 (85 percent) eligible blacks turned out to vote.[19]

BLACKS IN CONGRESS DURING RECONSTRUCTION

Two blacks won seats in the U.S. Senate (Hiram Revels and Blanche K. Bruce; both from Mississippi) and twenty won in the U.S. House. At least twelve of the blacks who were elected to Congress had formerly been slaves. From 1870 to the turn of the century, twenty-two African Americans served in the U.S. Congress.

The black members of Congress were all male, all from the South, and all members of the Republican Party. While a few blacks held elected offices in the North, the black community was too small in most northern congressional districts to be able to elect a black candidate.

The first black to be elected to Congress and seated was Hiram Rhodes Revels from Mississippi, who was elected to the U.S. Senate. Prior to the passage of the Seventeenth Amendment in 1913, U.S. Senators were elected by state legislatures rather than by popular vote. It is a notable historic irony that he was elected to fill the unexpired term of Jefferson Davis, the defeated president of the Confederacy. Revels was elected to the U.S. Senate on January 20, 1870, and took his seat on February 25. His views and general political behavior were conservative. Rather than fight for the extension of political rights for blacks, he advocated temperance and high moral standards as the keys to black freedom. Over time, Revels lost the support of many blacks and, in the state election of 1875, he had become so disenchanted with the Republican Party that he campaigned for some Democrats, a political blunder from which he never recovered.

Blanche Kelson Bruce of Mississippi, an ex-slave, was the first African American to serve a full term in the U.S. Senate. He was elected on March 5, 1875, and served until March 3, 1881. Bruce held several offices before coming to Congress. He fought to give blacks more land grants, sought to desegregate the army, and tried to help poor blacks who had left the South to find a better life in Kansas. Bruce also attempted to obtain more equitable treatment for American Indians. He left office in 1881. In 1888, Bruce's stature was so high that he received eleven votes for vice president at the Republican National Convention.[20]

Joseph Hayne Rainey, the first black member of the U.S. House of Representatives, was elected on December 12, 1870. Born a slave in Georgetown, South Carolina, he fled to Bermuda during the Civil War to escape being pressed into service by the Confederate government. In 1866, he returned to South Carolina and in 1870 he was elected to the U.S. House in a special election. Despite Democratic allegations of election fraud and racist efforts to unseat him, Rainey won reelection three times before being defeated in 1878.

BLACKS IN OFFICE AT THE STATE AND LOCAL LEVEL

The majority of blacks who held office during Reconstruction did so at the state and local levels. Blacks were involved from the very beginning in the rebuilding of the political structures in the South. About one thousand black delegates attended state constitutional conventions between 1867 and 1869 when the southern states were forced to reconstitute themselves along lines that were more democratic.

In some states where large numbers of blacks were concentrated in local political jurisdictions, it was inevitable that if blacks could vote they would elect their own. In practice this meant that the greater the number of blacks in a state, the greater the number of black elected officials to emerge. According to the 1870 census, in South Carolina, Mississippi, and Louisiana blacks were 50 percent or more of the state's population. As a result, more than half of the blacks who held office during this period came from these states.[21]

Conversely, in the southern states where blacks were the smallest percentage of the population—such as Arkansas, Tennessee, and Texas, where blacks were 25 percent or less of the population—they also had the least number of elected officials. There were few blacks elected in Arkansas, Tennessee, or Texas.

Blacks held twenty-five major state offices in the South. For blacks to win these offices, especially given that many of them were former slaves and generally uneducated, was remarkable. It meant that many whites, virtually all Republican, were willing to vote for and take leadership from blacks.

Blacks never controlled any particular state, though, for several reasons. First, although the federal Republican Party helped to put blacks in political offices to contain their white Democratic rivals in the states, at the same time, it hesitated to give too much authority to blacks. The image of black rule over whites was still a radical concept that few Republican leaders were willing to push too far.

Second, southern Democrats kept up a continual campaign of attacks on black Democrats and exploited the racist views and fears of many whites. Democrats referred to the new legislatures as "Monkey Houses" and spread fabricated stories of criminal behavior and incompetence on the part of black officeholders and their Republican backers. The mistakes of a few blacks were highlighted to condemn all blacks that held elected office. Republicans would not refute these charges. Third, the inexperience of blacks in both running for office and in executing the duties of office became factors.

The numbers of black elected officials were about evenly split between those who had been free and those who had been held in bondage. At least ten of the Reconstruction black officials were escaped slaves.

Surprisingly, the education level of the black politicians was relatively high and may have been higher overall than that of white elected officials. Roughly 83 percent, or 933, were literate. There were at least 237 ministers among the black officials, which reflected the continuing leadership of the black church that existed during slavery. At least 172 teachers were represented among black politicians. In many ways, the Reconstruction period was the heyday of black political power in the

United States. Average African Americans were engaged in nearly every area of political life in important and often decisive ways. That millions of ex-slaves within a few short years could reach such a plateau was extraordinary—and threatening. This situation would soon come to an end.

THE DEATH OF RECONSTRUCTION

"This, Mr. Chairman, is perhaps the Negroes' temporary farewell to the American Congress; but let me say, Phoenix-like he will rise up some day and come again. These parting words are in behalf of an outraged, heart-broken, bruised, and bleeding, but God-fearing people, faithful, industrious, loyal people—rising people, full of potential force."

North Carolina Representative George White's farewell speech to Congress ushering in a twenty-eight-year absence of blacks in Congress, January 29, 1901.[22]

The Hayes-Tilden southern compromise finished Reconstruction. In the presidential election of 1876, Democratic candidate Samuel J. Tilden won the popular vote but Republican candidate, Rutherford B. Hayes, won the electoral college by one vote—185 to 184.

Finally, an electoral commission established to settle the dispute, voted (on a party line) eight-to-seven for Hayes. This ignited a filibuster by southern Democrats in Congress. On February 2, 1877, Hayes and the southerners negotiated a deal. The southern Democrats would stop the filibuster and, in exchange, Hayes, who would be president, would give the South "Home Rule," withdraw federal troops from the region, and increase the allocation of money to southern businesses. Under Home Rule, Hayes was permitting the South to ignore the rights of blacks with little worry of federal interference.[23] On April 10, 1877, Hayes withdrew the troops from Columbia, South Carolina, indicating once and for all the end of Reconstruction.

BLACK POLITICAL POWER DESTROYED

Within an extraordinarily short time, black political power in the South was demolished. Blacks in local government were either voted out or violently removed by gangs of whites. Many were beaten and killed. In Congress and at the state and local levels, few Republicans spoke out against the attacks on blacks. The constitutions that had been drawn up only a few short years earlier were rewritten. Mississippi rewrote its constitution in 1888, followed by South Carolina (1898), North Carolina (1901), Alabama (1901), Virginia (1902), and Georgia (1908).[24]

Never a friend of blacks, the Supreme Court overturned civil rights legislation and sanctioned violations of the the Thirteenth, Fourteenth, and Fifteenth Amendments. In 1896, in the infamous *Plessey v. Ferguson* case, the Supreme Court ruled that the South could practice "separate but equal" treatment of blacks both in private and public affairs. It was clear, however, that the reality was separate and highly unequal.

Under the banner of states' rights, southerners passed laws that nullified the Fourteenth and Fifteenth Amendment rights and voting rights of blacks. J. Morgan Kousser identifies at least sixteen registration and voting tactics that created obstacles used by southern whites (and often by those in the North) to deny blacks the right to vote.[25]

Many of these schemes, such as the literacy test and poll tax, also initially disenfranchised many whites. To circumvent a potential political crisis of white support, the "grandfather clause" option was invented. Under this law, anyone whose grandfather voted before the Civil War was exempted from taking a literacy test. If voting had already occured in a person's family, did they somehow inherit political responsibility and insight? The point was to block the voting strength of the only ones whose grandfathers had not voted before the war—the blacks. In 1915, in *Guinn v. United States*, the Supreme Court outlawed the grandfather clauses.

At this point, three of the most effective tactics were the poll tax, literacy tests, and the all-white primary. These maneuvers would all eventually be overturned by Supreme Court decisions, but only after many, many years of damage.

The Poll Tax

Poll taxes had begun to disappear in the years prior to the Civil War. They came roaring back, however. As one member of the 1890 Mississippi Constitutional Convention's Franchise Committee stated, the poll tax was "the most effective instrumentality of Negro disfranchisement."[26]

Newly-arrived white ethnic immigrants were also targeted. Thus, the poll tax reflected an ethnic and class bias as well. In the eleven southern states, the total number of potential voters of *all* races not voting because of the poll tax was an estimated 7,700,000.[27]

Yet, in the South, blacks were the main focus. Not until 1966, in *Harper v. Virginia Board of Elections*, did the Supreme Court finally ban the poll tax, stating that it violated "equal protection of the laws" as guaranteed by the Fourteenth Amendment.[28]

Literacy Tests

Literacy tests for voting of any sort are an affront to democracy. In the South, however, this practice was taken to a level of unheard of absurdity. Blacks were asked questions that certainly their questioners could not have answered and, indeed, probably few scholars in the nation could either. For example, blacks would be asked "How many bubbles in a bar of soap?"[29] or "How many windows in the White House?"[30] In Alabama, a "voter" had to "Read, write, understand, and explain any section of the U.S. Constitution, to the satisfaction of county board of registrars."[31] In Georgia, the applicant must give a 'reasonable interpretation' of any paragraph of the Constitution of the U.S. or Georgia when read by one of the registrars.[32] In practice, white registrars simply asked whatever questions they could dream of and blacks had little recourse. It was not until the 1965 Voting Rights Act that literacy tests of any kind were banned.

All-White Primaries
The purpose of the all-white primaries was to allow whites to choose which candidates would end up in the general election. At best, blacks could only vote for the white candidates they had no role in choosing. White-only primaries came to an end on April 3, 1944, when the Supreme Court, by an eight-to-one margin, ruled in *Smith v. Allwright,* that they were illegal. Southern segregationists were outraged. Senator Burnet R. Maybank of South Carolina stated, "Regardless of the Supreme Court decision and any laws that may be passed by Congress, we in South Carolina are going to do whatever we can to protect our white primaries."[33]

As a result of all these machinations, blacks in the South were profoundly disenfranchised. In Louisiana, in 1896, there were 130,334 registered black voters; in 1900, there were 5,320, and by 1904, there were only 1,342.[34] Black elected officials at all levels disappeared.

CHAPTER THREE

The All-Black Towns Movement

At the same time as Reconstruction was coming to an end, the building of the railroads across the continent was opening the western lands to settlers. Blacks were among the pioneers who rode in wagons and on horseback to Oklahoma, Texas, Kansas, and even as far as California. Their goal was not only to escape the racial ravages of the South, but also to build all-black towns where they would be able to govern their own affairs through town meetings, regular elections, and political debate. Nationalist leaders, such as Benjamin "Pap" Singleton and Edwin P. McCabe, unlike the emigrationist leaders of the past, proposed that all-black enclaves could be built inside of the United States.

White land developers and railroad agents foresaw the profit in building towns around potential rail lines. They were willing to risk capital in purchasing the land and then recruiting settlers. The speculators tapped into the frustration felt by blacks in the South and sent black agents to the South to encourage migration.

Oklahoma

Historian Arthur Lincoln Tolson estimates that there were about twenty-seven all-black towns in Oklahoma dating from the 1850s. Thousands of blacks moved to Oklahoma in the 1880s from Texas, Georgia, Arkansas, Mississippi, Louisiana, and Tennessee. The goal was to make Oklahoma an all-black state. Numerous references were made to Oklahoma as the "land of the Negro."[1]

The all-black group, the First Grand Independent Brotherhood (FGIB), headquartered in Nicodemus, Oklahoma, distributed buttons and flyers nationwide in its effort to recruit blacks to the state. One of its projects was the creation of the Oklahoma Immigration Association. FGIB took a militant posture and stated, "The white man will only be tolerated because of his business qualifications." Firmly believing that it was possible to develop a black state, FGIB outlined an ambitious program and platform. It sought to fill all political offices in the state with blacks, allow only black teachers to teach, and force mixed racial attendance (including Native Americans) in the public schools.

In 1890, according to estimates, there were twenty thousand blacks in Oklahoma compared with about twenty-five thousand whites. To prevent blacks from playing a significant role as Oklahoma strove to become a state (which was achieved in 1907), whites eventually had to disenfranchise the black population.

The Afro-American Colonialization Company and the Colored Immigration Bureau also recruited blacks to Oklahoma. A direct link existed between lynching violence against blacks and the migration movement. In 1890, three black men—Tom Moss, Will Stewart, and Calvin McDowell—were lynched in Tennessee. Immediately, a meeting was held of two thousand blacks denouncing the lynchings and vowing to leave for Oklahoma. This panicked white businessmen and farmers because it occurred at the beginning of agriculture season when many white farmers were dependent on (cheap) black labor.

Many who left for the all-black towns bettered their condition. One researcher found that in one town, blacks had bank deposits ranging from two hundred dollars to one thousand dollars, an extraordinary amount in those days. A newspaper article lamented the fact that poor whites were in the position of having to ask for public assistance.

A key player in the effort to create what whites were calling derisively the "Negro state" was Edwin P. McCabe, the former auditor of the state of Kansas. McCabe, who had arrived in Oklahoma in 1889, was the principle founder of Langston, which became one of the most thriving of the all-black towns. He published the *Langston City Herald*, a newspaper that recruited blacks to the state and documented their lives and struggles.

McCabe, having plenty of black support, actually sought to become governor of the proposed black state. He said, "If I should be appointed governor, I would administer the laws in the United States without fear or favor to white or black alike."[2] McCabe's potential candidacy was vigorously opposed by whites from both major parties. One white Republican stated, "If McCabe is appointed governor . . . I would not give five cents for his life."[3]

His campaign sought support from African Americans from coast to coast. In April 1890, a delegation of twenty blacks from around the nation went to Washington and met with several administration officials, including President William Harrison, to lobby on McCabe's behalf. Blacks in Ohio, Illinois, New York, Indiana, Massachusetts, and Pennsylvania made known their support for McCabe and even threatened to switch their vote to the Democratic Party if he was not appointed. Eventually,

McCabe was appointed deputy territorial auditor by President Harrison.

McCabe, the head of the Colored Republicans of Logan County, was a loyal Republican active in organizing Republican clubs among blacks. He received support from the party because his efforts were consistent with the goals of the Republicans to make Oklahoma an overwhelming Republican state.

Whites in the state responded negatively to the all-black towns and to blacks in general. In the Oklahoma towns of Norman, Sapulpa, and Waurika, signs were posted that warned blacks they had twenty-four hours to get out of town. In Claremore, blacks were physically driven out. Jim Crow laws began to appear in the 1890s and became so extensive that even phone booths became segregated.

In some instances, blacks responded in-kind. In some of the all-black towns, white visitors were accepted but not encouraged to stay around. In Wybark, whites reportedly were not allowed to stay in town after dark.[4] In other towns, the title of lots could not pass to any whites and no whites were allowed to conduct business or reside in the town.

Green I. Currin, Oklahoma's first black elected state legislator, joined the Territorial Legislative Assembly on August 28, 1890. Currin's legislative initiatives included introducing a civil rights bill, House Bill No. 119, officially titled "An Act for the Protection of the Civil Rights of Citizens of the Terrortory."[5] The bill, which called for a penalty of one thousand dollars for those who violated the civil rights of others, did not pass.

As late as 1905, when blacks were virtually locked out of public service and unable to vote across the entire South, some blacks were able to get elected to political office in racially-mixed towns. In the Muskogee election of 1905, a Mr. Sims, a black man whose first name is lost to posterity, was elected tax collector along with a slate of whites who favored voting and civil rights for blacks.[6]

POLITICS IN THE ALL-BLACK TOWNS

Although citizens of all-black towns welcomed the opportunity to elect their own officials, many of the towns instituted the same restrictions on voting that existed in the broader society. Women were denied the right to vote in elections although it is believed that some held office. In at least one town, Clearview, only those who owned property could vote. Most of these restrictions fell away over time.[7]

Black town residents appeared to be eager to participate in the electoral process. Registration and turnout rates, uninhibited by racial violence and harassment, were extremely high. In Boley, the turnout rate averaged 80 percent, which was even higher than in most white areas. Despite the refusal to let women vote, the all-black towns were vanguards of democracy. They encouraged people to vote by eliminating advance voter registration and using secret ballots, which were rare practices in other parts of the United States.

Residents of the all-black towns strongly supported the Republican Party: often 70 percent or more of the eligible voters were registered as Republicans. The Democratic Party had few followers in these towns. In Nicodemus, for example, the Democratic Party won only fifteen votes in the nine presidential elections between 1880 and 1912.[8] As one writer noted, the terms "Democrat" and "race prejudice" were seen as synonymous.[9]

Several political parties attempted to challenge the domination of the Republican Party. In Boley, the Citizens Party and the Peoples Party both vied for the vote. The Populist Party was present in several of the all-black towns and a national spokesperson visited a few of them.

While the party never gained ground in most of the towns, it made a respectable showing in presidential elections in the township of Nicodemus where its candidate won 35 percent of the vote in 1892 and 39 percent in 1896.[10]

Most of the all-black towns had a mayor-council-type of government, and a marshal, justice of the peace, treasurer, assessor, and town clerk. Town meetings were held to discuss various issues, from closing down speakeasies to concerns about security and economic development. Unfortunately for the all-black towns, government power at the local level rested in the county seat and none of the black towns, though they tried valiantly, was ever designated a county seat. Whoever controlled the county seat more or less controlled funds. Decisions on where schools would be built, where sewage systems and electricity would be laid, and where hospital construction would be subsidized were made by county supervisors and not local town mayors or city councils. Due to white control of the ballot boxes and gerrymandering, blacks were unable to win enough votes to control any county seat. All-black towns were reduced to supporting white towns that appeared to be friendly.

Distrust and factionalism were rampant in the all-black towns according to historian Norman Crockett. He argues that because race was no longer a uniting factor, fierce battles took place over policy differences and minor disagreements could be blown up into major fights. In the town of Boley for instance, disputes often became so hostile that outside mediators would be asked to intercede. In one instance, Boley sought the counsel of civil rights leader Booker T. Washington. However, Washington steadfastly refused to visit the black towns where residents were fighting publicly among themselves. Most black town citizens and leaders were firm believers in the Booker T. Washington philosphy of self-help and social separation from whites, and Washington in turn was a big booster of the all-black town movement. These self-help efforts were in sync with his views that blacks could make it on their own, apart from whites. Yet while praising the bootstrap philosophy of these towns, Washington was silent on the political and economic attacks that they had to endure. He did not use his influence with either the white media or the White House to bring some relief to his followers.

Hostility toward the all-black towns grew in the first decade of this century as a number of towns passed Jim Crow laws. Many all-white towns—known as "sunshine towns"—enacted statutes that forbade blacks to be inside their town limits after sundown. The white newspapers were central in building an antagonistic atmosphere toward blacks. In Oklahoma, one white newspaper, *Weleetka American,* was especially provocative in its attacks on blacks. One of its headlines blared,

---

STOP! LOOK! LISTEN!
TO A RAILROAD DANGER SIGNAL!
THE COUNTY IS IN DANGER OF NEGRO DOMINATION —
WHITE VOTERS, CRUSH THE INSOLENCE OF THE NEGRO!
PROTECT YOUR HOMES WITH YOUR BALLOT![11]

Blacks in Oklahoma were not exempt from the type of racist terror that many thought they had left behind in the South. By 1907, when Oklahoma formally became a state, at least one black had been lynched and violence against blacks and their properties was growing.

By 1910, in Oklahoma and other states where all-black towns were located, disenfranchisement outside of the towns was nearly complete. In some areas, poll taxes, grandfather clauses, literacy tests, perpetual relocation of poll sites, and other devices were used to eliminate the black voter from county and state elections. When these methods did not work, violence was employed. In 1911, Paden, Oklahoma, residents Laura Nelson and her teenage son, who were being falsely accused of murder, were forcefully seized from the local jail in Okemah and lynched. Mrs. Nelson was raped repeatedly before being killed.[12]

Unfortunately, some blacks collaborated with Democrats in their campaigns to disenfranchise other blacks, as in the example of Isaiah T. Montgomery, one of the founders of the all-black town Mound Bayou in Mississippi. In July 1890, on the Republican ticket, Montgomery and George Melchoir, a white man, were elected to represent Bolivar County, Mississippi, at the state's Constitutional Convention. Although the official reason for the convention was to clean up government corruption, its real purpose was to disenfranchise black voters. Montgomery was the only black and only state Republican in attendance at a convention dominated by 130 Democrats.

Rather than denounce the convention and its vile intent, Montgomery joined the conspirators. He sat on the Committee on Franchise, Apportionment and Elections that recommended the institution of a state literacy test. The test, to be applied at the discretion of the local election judge, asked the prospective voter to give a "reasonable interpretation" of the U.S. Constitution. The Democrats who crafted this scheme had no doubt about who would take the test. This plan, when implemented, would eliminate at least 124,000 blacks from the registration rolls, ensuring white control of the state and most local areas.

Most troublesome, however, Montgomery's speech at the convention rivals Washington's ignoble 1895 "Atlanta Compromise" address in its concession to white racism. In the speech, Montgomery defended, indeed celebrated, the disenfranchisement of blacks. He stated that blacks had failed to reach the "high plane of moral, intellectual, and political excellence" achieved by whites. His hour-long oration praised white slaveholders by referring to them as "the proudest aristocracy that ever graced the Western hemisphere."[13] In a 1904 letter to Washington, Montgomery confessed that he regretted making the speech and that it was one of the great political blunders of his life.[14]

The damage had been done, however. Whites could find no better cover for their political deeds than to have a black leader endorse their actions. While white newspapers praised Montgomery's words, black editors criticized him fiercely. Booker T. Washington, at the time, made no comments on Montgomery's statements.

Some black leaders in the towns began to argue that blacks should minimally split their allegiance between the major parties. S. Douglas Russell, for example, the editor of the *Western Age in Langston*,[15] had argued as early as the 1880s that blacks should consider the Democratic Party. By the end of the first decade of the twentieth century, blacks in many areas of the South, including the all-black towns, had little choice but to vote Democratic. While party affiliation tended to matter little in the all-black towns, it was decisive in the county and state elections. The control of the ballot box often meant that even those few blacks who were allowed to vote had to vote Democratic or risk being turned away from the polls on the ground that they were Republicans. Realizing that Republicans no longer held sway in the southern states, the few blacks who could still vote opted for the practical solution of choosing among the various Democratic contenders.

CHAPTER FOUR

The Fight for Black Political Power, 1900—1965

In the first two decades of this century, the refusal of the Republicans to pass antilynching legislation and to address the poverty of the black community frustrated blacks. While some leaders supported radical third parties, others advocated building an alliance with the Democrats. In the South, this proposal had little legitimacy. In the North, however, the Democrats appeared more sensitive to black concerns than Republicans who held power but did very little.

As early as 1911 black members of the Democratic Party urged blacks to "cease following any one party to their detriment and thus divide their votes."[1] However, blacks continued to vote overwhelmingly Republican up until the 1930s.

FROM THE PARTY OF LINCOLN TO THE PARTY OF FDR.

The turning point in black party relations occurred during the Franklin Delano Roosevelt administrations. Roosevelt created numerous programs and initiatives during the Depression that benefited African Americans including the Works Projects Administration (WPA), work and home relief, farm loans, school lunches, public housing, and a minimum wage. Roosevelt's programs created enough of a distinction between the Democrats and the Republicans to push the majority of the blacks to vote for Roosevelt in 1936.

In 1932, when Roosevelt first ran, he received only scant support from black voters in the North. Things changed dramatically in the next four years. In the 1936 contest, where the black vote became Democratic, Roosevelt won 71 percent of the nation's black vote. In Chicago, his black vote doubled to 49 percent.[2]

In 1940, Roosevelt won 67 percent of the black vote.[3] The party platform included a strong statement against racism. It said, "We have aided more than half-a-million Negro youths in vocational training, education, and employment. We shall continue to strive for complete legislative safeguards against discrimination in government services and benefits, and in the national defense forces. We pledge to uphold due process and equal protection of laws for every citizen, regardless of race, creed, or color."[4]

In 1944 Roosevelt squared off against Thomas Dewey. In that election, "blacks provided a key margin of victory for Roosevelt in Pennsylvania, Maryland, Michigan, Missouri, New York, Illinois, and New Jersey."[5] Political analyst Henry Lee Moon argues that in 1944, "In sixteen states with a total of 278 votes in the electoral college, the Negro, in a close election, may hold the balance of power; that is, in an election in which the non-Negro vote is about evenly divided."[6] In four states—Wisconsin, Ohio, New Jersey, and Michigan—the margin of difference was less than 1 percent of the vote. In three states—Pennsylvania, Missouri, and Illinois—the difference was less than 2 percent.[7]

By 1946, many blacks were feeling frustrated with the Democratic Party. Having just completed a war to liberate Europe, black Americans wanted freedom at home. Neither Republicans nor Democrats were perceived by African Americans as strong advocates of racial equality. Many voted Republican in the mid-term elections or not at all. As a consequence of low black turnout, vote switching, and dissatisfaction by others in the Democratic coalition, the Republicans took Congress for the first time since 1930.[8]

In 1948, blacks were key to Harry Truman's win. Truman was popular among many blacks due to his creation of the Fair Employment Board within the Civil Service Commission, and the outlawing of segregation in the armed services.[9] At the Democratic convention that year, hard-core segregationist Strom Thurmond and other southern states' rights advocates left the convention immediately after Truman's nomination and within days had formed the States' Rights Party whose mission was to siphon off white southern votes from Truman. Earlier in the year, the Democratic Party had split to the left when Wallace and his supporters among liberals, labor, and blacks departed and formed the Progressive Party. Abandoned by the party's right and left, Truman had little choice but to frantically seek black support.

Fearful that the popular Dewey could win, especially if Wallace was able to pull black and labor votes, Truman made deals with the NAACP and pledged to support civil rights legislation, promote fair employment procedures, and push for more rapid desegregation with federal contractors.[10] Walter White, head of the NAACP, aggressively urged blacks not to support Wallace, the Progressive Party candidate.

Even with these efforts, black support for Truman was not universal. The only major black newspaper to endorse Truman was the *Chicago Defender*.[11] Dewey and Wallace's effort to court blacks paid off to some degree. For example, the *Amsterdam News*, one of the most influential black-oriented newspapers of the time, gave its endorsement to Dewey, noting his appointment of blacks. Others black leaders, such as New York City Councilman and openly communist Benjamin Davis and the radical intellectual W. E. B. Du Bois, considered Truman a racist and backed Wallace. Activist and artist Paul Robeson was vice chairman of Wallace's Progressive Party and even superstar boxer Joe Louis made contributions to the campaign.[12] At one rally for Wallace in Harlem, fifteen thousand blacks turned out.[13]

Truman also went to Harlem. On October 29, he spoke at a gathering in the famed African American community, the first U.S. president to do so. He said, "Our determination to attain the goal of equal rights and equal opportunity must be resolute and unwavering."[14]

Although he won the bulk of the black vote, Truman's views on blacks were profoundly prejudiced. He held deeply personal racist attitudes before, during, and after his terms in office. His private letters contained some of the most vicious racial slurs ever recorded by any president. In one letter he wrote in 1911 to his future wife Bess, he stated, "I think one man is just as good as another so long as he's honest and decent and not a nigger or a Chinaman. Uncle Will says that the Lord made a White man from dust, a nigger from mud, then he threw up what was left and it came down a Chinaman."[15] In other letters during his presidency, he referred to blacks who worked in the White House as "an army of coons" and discussed what he called "nigger picnic day."[16]

A Gallup poll taken in the early 1950s found that the black vote had become Democratic. According to the poll,

W. E. B. Du Bois

a slight majority of blacks identified themselves as Democrats: 54 percent Democrats, 23 percent Republicans, and 23 percent Independents. Despite these numbers, the black vote for Republican president Dwight Eisenhower grew from 20 percent in 1952 to 38 percent by 1956.[17]

At the same time, an angry number of blacks were expressing their displeasure with Truman's policies. Congressman Charles Diggs from Detroit was sharply critical of the Democrats and supported Eisenhower. So did Congressman Adam Clayton Powell who stomped for Eisenhower. Powell, who was called a "republicrat,"[18] stated that "I must commit what could be called political suicide and throw my support to President Eisenhower."[19]

In 1952, more than one million blacks were registered in the South (See Table 1, page 47). Yet, little voting and virtually no office-holding took place. In Mississippi, the lack of high registration was celebrated by white state leaders. Out of five hundred thousand blacks eligible to vote, only fifteen hundred were actually registered and even most of those dare not attempt to vote. Governor Theodore Bilbo, a staunch segregationist, stated, "The best way to keep a nigger away from a white primary is to see him the night before."[20] In 1958, at the "Conference on Voting Restrictions in Southern States," it was noted that not more than 25 percent of the six million voting age blacks in the South were registered.[21]

BLACK ELECTED OFFICIALS AFTER 1945

While African Americans in the South were fighting for the right to vote, an increasing number of blacks were winning offices and appointments in the Midwest, the Northeast, and in Washington, D.C. By the mid-1940s, blacks began to get elected to Congress, state offices, city councils and school boards across the country including the southern states of Virginia, North Carolina, and Ten-

TABLE I:
BLACK VOTER REGISTRATION IN
THE SOUTH—1940–1973

YEAR	NUMBER REGISTERED	PERCENTAGE REGISTERED
1940	250,000	5
1947	595,000	12
1952	1,008,614	20
1956	1,233,038	25
1960	1,414,052	28
1964	1,907,279	38
1968	3,312,000	62
1970	3,357,000	54
1971	3,488,565	59
1973	3,560,856	59

Source: E. Yvonne Moss with Tobe Johnson, Dianne M. Pinderhughes, Michael B. Preston, Susan Welch, and John F. Zipp, "Black Political Participation: The Search for Power," in Wornie L. Reed, ed., African-American: Essential Perspectives (Westport, CT: Auburn House, 1993), p. 84.

nessee. In 1946, two black congressional candidates, Chicago's William Dawson and New York's Adam Clayton Powell, both won their races.

In 1949, Theodore Berry was elected the first black city council member in Cincinnati, Ohio. Berry's political heights hit a racial ceiling, however. Although he won the highest vote total in 1953 and 1955, he was not selected to be mayor as was tradition in the city. He subsequently was selected to be vice mayor.[22] Nationwide, there were more than two dozen blacks in state legislatures in New York, Massachusetts, Pennsylvania, New Jersey, Vermont, Illinois, Kansas, Nebraska, California, Colorado, West Virginia, and Kentucky. In 1946, in New York, as an impressive statement of the rising black political power, a black communist, Benjamin J. Davis, was elected to the New York City Council. In 1953, also in New York, Hulan Jack became the Manhattan Borough President. Jack, an emigrant from St. Lucia, was paid $25,000, oversaw a budget of $5 million, and managed 1,415 employees—a significant amount of responsibility for an African American during that period.[23]

In 1950, black historian, scholar, and open Socialist W. E. B. Du Bois ran for the U.S. Senate in New York in a three-month campaign on the American Labor Party ticket. Hesitant to run at first, Du Bois decided to enter the race, with limited effort given his age, because he would be able to discuss peace and civil rights issues as well as help the campaign of progressive congressman Vito Marcantonio. In his minimal campaign, Du Bois gave only ten speeches and delivered seven broadcasts. Most the rallies that he participated in brought out between one thousand and twenty-five hundred people, although at the last rally of the campaign, held on October 24 at Madison Square Garden, more than seventeen thousand people attended.

Du Bois ascribed his loss as due to the inability of his campaign to financially compete with the campaign of the major parties. As he sharply stated, "Anyone who thinks that money does not buy American elections is a fool."[24] In the end, he received 205,729 votes, 4 percent of the votes cast. He won 15 percent of the Harlem vote.[25] Du Bois was soon to find out that his radicalism, even at the age of eighty-one, was not appreciated in conservative circles. In February 1951, two months after the election, he was indicted on charges of being an "agent of a foreign principal" for his work with the peace information center.[25]

By 1960, blacks constituted ten of thirty-three seats on the Cleveland City Council and six of twenty-eight seats on the St. Louis City Council. In St. Louis, blacks were two of twelve on the school board. Even in some southern cities, such as Nashville, Memphis, and Louisville, blacks began to win seats in municipal government.[26]

The Democrats took back the White House in 1960 with the victory of President John F. Kennedy. Most civil rights black leaders at the time, such as Rev. Martin Luther King, Jr., took a nonpartisan stance and gave no official support to either Kennedy or Republican candidate Richard Nixon. However, some analysts believe that the election may have been won by a single phone call. To stop his activism, King had been arrested in Georgia for technically not possessing a driver's license. It was suggested to Kennedy that he call King's wife, Coretta, to boost his black support. Although Kennedy first resisted because he was afraid of alienating the white southern vote, on October 26, he made the phone call that was heard around the black world. As word spread throughout the black community, Kennedy's black support solidified. Martin Luther King, Sr., who had been supporting Nixon, announced that he was switching his vote.

Nixon had been advised by his campaign team not to call King or to aggressively seek the black vote—to his regret. "I could have become President," stated Nixon, "I needed only five percent more votes in the Negro areas. I could have gotten them if I had campaigned harder."[27]

In spite of the gains mentioned above, the denial of voting rights for most African Americans would last until the mid-1960s when the Voting Rights Act was passed. The passage of that legislation would bring forth an era of black voting participation unseen in nearly 100 years.

CHAPTER FIVE

Black Members of Congress,
1928–1965

In the period between the two World Wars blacks migrated from the South to the North and the majority of black voters shifted to the Democratic Party—a change that would have profound political consequences. Jim Crow segregation, enforced by law and paramilitary bands, made life for blacks in the South a daily horror. Blacks were restricted in terms of where they could live, whom they could marry, what kind of jobs they could get, and what schools they could attend. In Atlanta, Georgia, black barbers were not allowed to cut white children's and women's hair; in Birmingham, Alabama, blacks and whites playing "dominoes or checkers" together was outlawed.[1]

The violence drove African Americans out of the South. Between 1882 and 1930, 1,663 blacks were lynched in Alabama, Georgia, Louisiana, Mississippi, and South Carolina. The legal violence was almost as lethal. White southern justice executed 1,299 blacks in those years.[2] Following World War I, in the summer of 1919, known as "Red Summer," seventy blacks were killed in race riots across the South and in other regions. This included ten black soldiers, some murdered in uniform, who had just returned from fighting in Europe.

While these conditions alone were enough to encourage many blacks to leave the South, there were also strong pulls from particular northern cities. In Chicago, Pittsburgh, Detroit, New York, and Cleveland, the industrial spurt of the 1920s and then the war-driven 1940s, meant there was a labor shortage, and one source of relatively cheap labor was blacks in the South. Henry Ford's offer of five dollars a day wage was irresistible to blacks who may have earned five dollars a *month* or, in many cases, just sank deeper and deeper in debt. Ford Motor Company and many other enterprises were willing to send trucks to the South to pickup and move new workers to the cities of the North. Blacks in Alabama went directly north to Detroit or Cleveland; blacks in Mississippi and Arkansas hit Route 50 to Chicago; and blacks in North Carolina and South Carolina migrated to New York, Philadelphia, and Pittsburgh.

In the first half of the twentieth century, the South lost more than three million blacks. Shifts also occurred within the South when "the percent of southern blacks living in urban places grew from 17 percent in 1900 to 33 percent by 1930."[3] The most critical shifts, however, were the migrations to the northern cities, especially New York, Detroit, Philadelphia, and Chicago. From 1910 to 1920, the black population grew in Detroit by 611 percent, in Philadelphia by 500 percent, and in Chicago by 148 percent.[4] Between 1910 and 1940 the black population in the North had more than doubled.[5]

Black majorities or near majorities in Chicago, Detroit, Philadelphia, and New York started to elect blacks to school boards, city councils, and beginning in 1928, to Congress. Chicago would have the unique distinction of electing both the first black Republican mem-

TABLE II:
BLACK MIGRATION OUT OF THE SOUTH

Year	Number of Blacks That Left
1900–1910	170,000
1910–1920	450,000
1920–1930	750,000
1930–1940	349,000
1940–1950	1,599,000
Total	**3,318,000**

Source: Stewart E. Tolnay and E. M. Beck, "Rethinking the Role of Racial Violence in the Great Migration," Alferdteen Harrison, ed., Black Exodus: The Great Migration from the American South (Jackson, MS: University Press of Mississippi, 1991), p. 20; Manning Marable, Race, Reform and Rebellion: The Second Reconstruction in Black America, 1945–1982 (Jackson, MS: University Press of Mississippi, 1984), pp. 8–9.

ber of Congress in the twentieth century and the first black Democratic member of Congress in any century.

This pull of African Americans to the cities, according to economist Harold Baron, initiated "the formation of a distinct black proletariat in the urban centers at the very heart of the corporate-capitalist process of production."[6] The collective consciousness that arose out of this process of change would be critical.

BLACK MEMBERS OF CONGRESS 1928–1965

Oscar De Priest (1928–1934)
Republican Oscar De Priest was elected in 1928 from Chicago, the first black member of the U.S. House of Representatives in this century. Born only six years after the end of the Civil War, the former house painter and

Oscar De Priest

real estate entrepreneur rose up quickly in the tough street politics of Chicago.

In 1915, De Priest won a city council seat, but was forced to resign after being indicted on charges of accepting protection money. With the renowned Clarence Darrow as his defense attorney, he won a dramatic acquittal. In November 1928 he became the first black elected to Congress outside of the South.

Upon his arrival in Congress, two southern representatives refused to have offices next to him. The Hoover adminstration was denounced across the South for inviting Mrs. De Priest to a social gathering at the White House. Although De Priest challenged segregation within Congress, such as its rigidly segregated dining facilities, little changed as a result of his protests.

During his short tenure, De Priest attempted to address race issues. He argued unsuccessfully that Congress should reduce the number of seats held by southern states that refused to let blacks vote. He also proposed that a seventy-five dollar monthly pension be given to ex-slaves above the age of seventy-five. This proposal was also defeated. Finally, he also proposed antilynching law as would virtually all subsequent black members.

Arthur Mitchell (1934–1942)

Arthur Mitchell's 1934 victory over De Priest, by a margin of 27,963 to 24,820,[7] made him the first black Democrat to be elected to Congress. Ironically, Mitchell had started his political career as a Republican. His shift to the Democrats occurred during the general change, in the early days of the Depression, by blacks towards the Democratic Party.

During his four terms in Congress, Mitchell used the floor of the House to address the concerns of blacks in his district and around the country. He denounced the Italian invasion of Ethiopia, which was a major issue in the black community and one that other members of Congress would not address. He also fought losing battles to outlaw lynching, end poll taxes, and stop discrimination in labor and civil service.

Mitchell became a trusted ally of Roosevelt and was rewarded during the 1936 presidential campaign with highly visible roles. He served as western director of minority affairs for Roosevelt's reelection campaign effort. He also gave the seconding speech for Roosevelt at the 1936 Democratic Party convention. These efforts probably contributed to the historic shift of blacks to the Democratic Party in the 1936 election.

One of Mitchell's most significant contributions occurred outside of the legislative arena. In 1937, he was forced to move to the Jim Crow section of a railroad train that he was riding although he had two first class tickets. He sued the Rock Island and Pacific Railway and the case went all the way up to the Supreme Court. Mitchell argued the case himself and contended that interstate trains should be exempt from state segregation laws. In April 1941, *Mitchell v. United States et al.* was decided in favor of Mitchell. In its decision, the Court held that blacks had the same right to receive the same accommodations and treatment as whites. It would be another fifteen years, however, before the Interstate Commerce Commission would ban segregation on all interstate travel and in the public waiting rooms of train and bus stations.

William Dawson (1942–1970)
William Levi Dawson was a genuine political power broker. He entered Chicago politics as a Republican, where he lost a congressional bid in 1928, but later switched to the Democratic Party. In 1942, he won the congressional seat vacated by Arthur Mitchell. He would go on to serve in Congress for twenty-seven years. He came under criti-

William Dawson

cism from civil rights leaders and even from his staff for his reluctance to push a civil rights agenda. Dawson mainly dispensed patronage and ran a tight operation back in Chicago.

Adam Clayton Powell, Jr. (1944–1970)

One of the most memorable black members of Congress was Adam Clayton Powell, Jr., who represented Harlem from 1944 to 1970. In the 1930s, Powell built his reputation as an organizer and leader while serving as minister of the Abyssinian Baptist Church in Harlem. During the Depression, his church provided food, clothing, shelter, and temporary jobs to poor blacks and others who lived in the area. Powell organized movements that forced bus lines, utilities, telephone companies, retail stores, Harlem Hospital, and even the promoters of the 1939 World's Fair to hire and promote blacks. Powell was elected to Congress in 1944.

When he arrived in Washington, he found the city as well as Congress to be segregated much like any place in the South. "White only" signs in the halls of Congress applied to black Congress members as well as their staff and constituents. Powell ordered his staff to eat at the whites-only House restaurant and he took his black constituents to white-only places and conducted peaceful "sit-ins." At the time, nonwhites from other countries were allowed to eat in the House and Senate segregated dining establishments.[8]

Powell also fought energetically on the floor of Congress. He introduced legislation to outlaw lynching, to repeal the poll tax, and to end discrimination in the armed forces, housing, employment, and transportation. He consistently attached antidiscrimination clauses to many pieces of legislation, as a way of getting around the House power structure that prevented antidiscrimination bills from rising out of committee.

During the McCarthy period, when the House Un-American Activities Committee (HUAC) issued contempt citations against witnesses who refused to give information to the committee, Powell alone opposed it. He was on the losing end of a 370-to-1 and 357-to-2 vote (along with progressive New York representative Vito Marcantonio).[9] Although not a communist, Powell supported the communists' right to free speech because they were part of the antiracist fight. He stated, "There is no group in America, including the Christian church, that practices racial brotherhood one-tenth as much as the Communist Party."[10] Outside of Congress, Powell was active in both international and national events. He attended the famous 1955 Bandung Conference of African and Asian nations.

Though a Democrat, Powell became increasingly frustrated with the lack of support for antidiscrimination legislation by the Truman administration and House Democrats. In 1956 he supported the Republican nominee Dwight Eisenhower. This breach of loyalty angered other Democrats and it was not long before Powell found himself under attack from a number of angles. In 1958, he was indicted on tax evasion and fraud charges.[11] He went to trial in 1960 and was defended by prominent attorney Edward Bennett Williams, winning a mistrial after six weeks in court. One year later, the government dropped all charges against Powell.

Despite these problems, in 1961 he became chair of the Education and Labor Committee from which he was able to produce many pieces of legislation. However, he also came under loud criticism for his high rate of absentism and for the many trips that he took abroad.

At the same time, he was also facing slander charges. On February 25, 1960, in a speech, he accused a Mrs. Esther James of being a "bag woman" who carried payoff money from known gamblers to the police. He repeated

Adam Clayton Powell, Jr.

the charge on a television program and James filed suit. She won her case on April 3, 1963, primarily because Powell continually canceled and refused to appear in court even though he reportedly could back up, at least partially, his claim. A jury awarded James 211,500 dollars in damages which was later reduced to 46,500 dollars.[12] Rather than pay the slander judgement, Powell went into self-exile. Powell's enemies could smell blood. Not only was Powell's reputation in tatters, but his political power in Congress was also being attacked.

On January 9, 1967, the House Democratic Caucus stripped Powell of his Labor Committee chairmanship. Although the Judiciary Committee recommended that Powell only be censured, fined, and stripped of seniority, the full House voted 307-to-116 on March 1, 1967, to kick Powell out of Congress altogether. New York was thereby forced to hold a special election to fill his seat. The House had not counted on the strength of Powell's ties to his constituents. In the April 11 special election, Powell won the seat that had been his only a month earlier. Powell refused to take his seat continuing to protest his slander judgement. In November 1968, Powell won his twelfth term in office although his participation in Congress over the last few years had been virtually nil.

In January 1969, he refused to take his seat again this time because he opposed the House decision that had taken his seniority and chairman's seat. Powell took his case all the way to the Supreme Court, which eventually ruled that the House had acted unconstitutionally when it purged Powell from Congress in 1967. However, the Court ruled that the House did not have to give him back his seniority. The following year, in June 1970, after what had been an amazing series of comebacks, Powell's time ran out. He lost the primary race to Charles Rangel who would go on to win the seat in November. After his primary defeat, Powell tried to get on the ballot as an inde-

Charles Diggs, Jr.

pendent, but was unsuccessful. Upon his retirement from
Congress, Powell returned to minister at Abyssinian Baptist Church. On April 4, 1972, he died in Miami bringing
to closure a remarkable life.

Along with Powell, there were other black Congressmembers who were critical in the debates in Congress
concerning civil rights and other issues important to
African Americans. The four black Congressmembers
who came to Congress in the 1950s and early 1960s were

Robert Nix, Sr.

Charles Diggs, Jr., Robert Nix, Sr., Augustus Hawkins, and John Conyers.

Other African American Members of Congress
In 1954, Charles Diggs, Jr. was elected to Congress.[13] He sought to increase the minimum wage, provide relief to the unemployed, establish a federal agency for the handicapped, and create a youth conservation corps. He was also vocal in support of the 1957 Civil Rights Act. In 1969,

Detroit's Charles Diggs founded and became the first chairman of the Congressional Black Caucus. This honor was a logical outgrowth of his long activist career both inside of Congress and out.

On the House Foreign Affairs Committee and later as chairman of its Subcommittee on Africa, Diggs was an outspoken advocate for people in the developing world. Diggs was also extremely active on the domestic front for black rights. He was one of the three chairman of the historic 1972 National Black Political Assembly convention held in Gary, Indiana, along with Gary Mayor Richard Hatcher and black nationalist Imamu Amiri Baraka.

In 1972, Diggs became chairman of the House District of Columbia Committee, and was instrumental in the passage of the District of Columbia Self-Government and Governmental Reorganization Act in December 1973. Under "Home Rule" legislation, people in the city could finally elect their own mayor, city council, and school board. Unfortunately, Diggs's tenure in Congress would end sadly. In 1973, he was convicted of mail fraud and falsifying payroll forms. He resigned from Congress on June 3, 1980, and eventually spent time in prison.

In 1958, Robert Nelson Cornelius Nix, Sr., was Pennsylvania's first black member of Congress. Nix's career was generally uneventful. He did support the civil rights legislation of the 1960s and worked behind the scenes to try to save Adam Clayton Powell's seat.

Winning his seat in 1962, California's Augustus Freeman "Gus" Hawkins became the first black congressmember from the West. He rose to become chair of the powerful Committee on Education and Labor, where he authored many pieces of progressive legislation. He was instrumental in getting the Equal Employment Opportunity Commission in Title VII of the 1964 Civil Rights Act, and he also introduced bills addressing housing, employment practices, low-cost housing and disability insurance

John Conyers

legislation, and workmen's compensation provisions for domestic workers. Hawkin's most enduring legacy was the Full Employment and Balanced Growth Act of 1978, also known as the Humphrey-Hawkins Act, which sought to place responsibility for creating jobs on the federal government.

As a former factory worker, labor organizer, and attorney for the Detroit Trade Union Leadership Council, John Conyers came to Washington in 1964 with the firm belief that he was a representative of working people. Viewed by many as the most radical black member, Conyers was active in the civil rights and black power movements of the 1960s. He was one of few national black figures who opposed the Vietnam War early on, and he called for abolition of the House Un-American Activities Committee.

Perhaps Conyers's greatest political achievement was to eventually win passage of the Martin Luther King, Jr., national holiday bill. Offered soon after King's assassination in 1968, it took Conyers nearly 15 years to get the bill passed. Finally, in 1983, during the Reagan administration, the bill became law.

Given their small numbers, congressmen such as Powell and Conyers viewed themselves as advocates for the entire black community and not just their own constituents. In reality, however, millions of blacks were not represented in Congress and had few means to apply pressure to policy-makers at the national level.

It would require the political forces unleashed by the black movement of the 1960s and the passage of the 1965 Voting Rights Act to generate enough black members of Congress to begin to bring to a national forum the grievances of the black community. At the same time, the spurt in the number of black elected officials would also have important consequences at the local level. For black communities in the South who had been without effective political representation for nearly a century, the last half of the 1960s was a virtual second Reconstruction.

CHAPTER SIX

The 1965 Voting Rights Act

In the mid-1950s, few African Americans in the South were able to vote even though the right legally existed. It would take the life-and-death struggles of voting rights activists in the deep South to eventually win the passage of the 1965 Voting Rights Act to make that right a reality.

FANNIE LOU HAMER AND THE MISSISSIPPI FREEDOM SUMMER

In 1962 and 1963, the Council of Federated Organizations, a coalition of civil rights groups, began an assault on the practice in Mississippi of preventing blacks from voting. In the coalition were the Student Non-violent Coordinating Committee (SNCC), the Southern Christian Leadership Conference (SCLC), Congress of Racial Equality (CORE), and NAACP. Under the leadership of Robert Moses, voter registration chief for the council and head of the Mississippi branch of SNCC, the 1964 "Free-

Fannie Lou Hamer speaking to the 1964 Democratic National Convention

dom Summer" project began, bringing in black and white volunteers from around the country to organize black voter registration across the state.[1] One result of this drive was the formation of the Mississippi Freedom Democratic Party (MFDP) and the emergence of one of its leaders, Fannie Lou Hamer.[2]

A poor sharecropper most of her life, Hamer would rise to national prominence as her voice for equality rose above the brutal Mississippi racism. Born October 6, 1917, Hamer was the twentieth child of sharecroppers who had worked all their life on other people's plantations, as would Hamer herself. As Hamer tells it, she had never known that blacks could register and vote until she went to a mass meeting in 1962 chaired by Robert Moses. She immediately volunteered to go the next day and try to register to vote. Her group of eighteen was arrested at the courthouse—allegedly because the bus they came in on was too yellow!—and when she returned home to the plantation after being bailed out of jail, she was given the choice of either quitting the movement or leaving the farm. She left the farm that night and never went back to sharecropping. In her unyielding efforts to win voting rights she would be horribly beaten on a number of occasions, confront serious health and personal financial problems, and even politically challenge Martin Luther King, Jr.

The Mississippi Freedom Democratic party (MFDP) was founded in 1964 because the regular state Democratic Party excluded blacks. MFDP's goal was to become the official state delegation to the 1964 Democratic National Convention in Atlantic City. The MFDP sent sixty-eight delegates, including four whites, to Atlantic City, demanding that they be seated in place of the regular, all-white, state delegation. Fearing a white southern backlash, Democratic presidential nominee Lyndon Johnson first offered to allow the MFDP delegation to be seated as "honored guests" and that only three of the regular state delegation would be accepted. The MFDP adamantly refused what they considered "tokenism." Hamer testified at nationally televised hearings at the convention and in a riveting and emotional moment told of her beatings and the viciousness that blacks in Mississippi had to face simply for wanting to vote. Even before she could finish, the White House was flooded with telegrams and phone calls from blacks and whites supporting the MFDP. Embarrassed, Johnson offered a second compromise where two delegates from MFDP would be officially seated with the regular delegation.

Martin Luther King, Jr., and other civil rights leaders were used to try to convince the MFDP delegation not to create a situation that would split the Democrats and cause Johnson to lose the election to conservative Republican Barry Goldwater. In the end, no compromise was reached, the all-white delegation was seated, and the MFDP went home empty-handed although the Democratic Party pledged that no all-white delegations would be seated at future conventions. The MFDP did not go away quietly, however. It returned to Mississippi and continued its battles at the state, county, and local levels.

While the MFDP and King had similar goals, for example, winning voting rights, they employed different strategies. The MFDP sought to expose the unfairness of the Mississippi system to the nation and shame it into reform. King, on the other hand, was trying to get national passage of legislation that would enforce voting rights for blacks everywhere. It was his hope, and that of other national civil rights leaders, that with Johnson and his liberal vice president Hubert Humphrey in the White House, a voting rights bill would pass Congress and be signed within a year of the election. Johnson won the election, but his reluctance to aggressively push the legislation delayed the passage of the bill. The 1965 Alabama voting rights march from Selma to Montgomery, Alabama, tipped the balance.

THE SELMA MARCH AND THE BATTLE IN CONGRESS

January

In January 1965, when King announced that SCLC would begin a voter registration drive in Selma, only 335 of 15,115 potential blacks in the city were registered.[3] The voter registration office was opened only two days out of the month. Under the rough rule of Dallas County sheriff James Clark, Jr., voting rights activists had met hostility and violence. In February 1965, Jimmy Lee Jackson, a black civil rights worker, had been killed by local police. Reverend James Reeb, a white minister who was active in the struggle, was also murdered on the streets of Selma.

February 4

The tensions in Selma drew even Malcolm X to town. The young SNCC activists wanted to impress upon the local whites the seriousness of their intent to break the back of disenfranchisement, and who better to upset whites than the fiery ex-minister of the Nation of Islam, Malcolm X? For his part, Malcolm was deeply interested in what was going on in the South and he wanted to have a chance to talk to King. By the time Malcolm arrived to speak at Selma's Brown Chapel, on February 4, King was in jail. In his remarks, Malcolm stated, "The white people should thank Dr. King for holding people in check, for there are others who do not believe in these measures. But I'm not going to try to stir you up and make you do something you would have done anyway."[4]

Malcolm had to hurry back to New York and did not get to visit King in jail. In Harlem, fifteen days later, Malcolm was assassinated. Before he left Selma, however, he did leave a message with King's wife, Coretta. "Mrs. King, will you tell Dr. King that I had planned to visit with him in jail? I won't get a chance now because I've got to leave to get to New York in time to catch a plane for London where I'm to address the African Students' Conference. I want Dr. King to know that I didn't come to Selma to make his job difficult. I really did come thinking I could make it easier. If the white people realize what the alternative is, perhaps they will be more willing to hear Dr. King."[5]

March 7

As part of the registration campaign and to protest the murder of Jimmy Lee Jackson and the arrest of thousands of activists, it was proposed that a fifty-four mile march along Route 80 (the Jefferson Davis highway) be held on Sunday, March 7, 1965. Alabama governor George Wallace, a rigid opponent of civil rights, outlawed the march and sent state troopers to make sure that it did not happen. Although King had called for the march, he was absent on that day preferring to preach at his church in Atlanta. As the several hundred marchers crossed Selma's Edmund Pettus bridge, they were greeted on the other side by Sheriff Clark and his army of police who demanded that the marchers turn around. In the hesitation before a decision could be made, Clark and his troops waded into the crowd of men, women, and children with tear gas, horses, and flailing billy clubs. Hundreds were injured in an orgy of police violence as the news media captured it all on film.

March 10

"Bloody Sunday," as the March 7 police riot was now called, had an immediate political impact. As King rushed to Selma to plan another demonstration, President Johnson was deluged with calls to protect the demonstrators and to move swiftly to put before the Congress voting rights legislation. A second march, led by King, was held on March 10 with about three thousand participants. As this group crossed the bridge, they too were met by Clark, local deputies, and state troopers who again ordered the marchers to go back. Surprising everyone, after kneeling and praying, King told the group to retreat and return to their starting point. Outraged, SNCC activists and others denounced King as an "Uncle Tom" and a coward. This action by King damaged his reputation among many young people and probably hastened the break between the young SNCC workers and the older civil rights crowd.[6]

March 15

President Johnson spoke before Congress on March 15: "At times history and fate meet at a single time in a single place to shape a turning point in man's unending search for freedom. So it was at Lexington and Concord. So it was a century ago at Appomattox. So it was last week in Selma, Alabama."[7]

Efforts to end violations of black voting rights at the local and state levels had clearly failed miserably. Local prosecutors refused to go after registrars and local and state governments resisted changing discriminatory laws. On the rare occasion that a discriminatory statute was removed by the courts, local or state officials would simply pass another similar law. It became obvious to voting rights activists and to the Johnson administration that only a law with federal force behind it could address the situation.

March 19

Johnson sent a bill to Congress March 19, authorizing the federal government, under certain circumstances, to intervene with federal examiners from the Justice Department in local voting situations. These federal examiners would have the authority to supersede local registrars and their powers if discrimination was found. Riding the winds of the Pettus Bridge incident, Johnson had momentum and even support from some congressional Republicans. Minority leader Senator Everett Dirksen (R-IL) supported the legislation and worked with congressional Democrats and the White House to push the bill through Congress.

Resistance to the bill from southern members was immediate and intense. Senator Sam Ervin (D-NC) argued that "states' rights" would be violated by the bill. Senator Leander Perez (D-LA) contended that the bill favored communists and "immoral" blacks.[8]

March 21

Finally, on March 21, about fifty thousand people from around the nation gathered in Selma. The marchers were of all races and backgrounds. Led by King and protected by federal and state police, they completed the march to the Montgomery State Capitol. In his speech at the rally, King stated that "no tide of racism can stop us."[9] Selma was the last great march of that era.

April 9

Back in the Senate, the bill was reported out of the Senate Judiciary Committee on April 9. Led by Senator James Eastland (D-MS), southern Democrats led a filibuster against the bill. Rather than call for an immediate vote to stop the filibuster, Johnson and the Senate leadership allowed a short period for the southerners to rant and then, on May 25, called for the cloture vote and won that vote by a 70 to 30 margin.[10] On May 26, Bill S. 1564 passed by 78 to 18, with three southerners and seven northern Republicans joining the Democratic backers of the bill.[11]

On the House side, notorious segregationist Howard Smith (D-VA), chair of the Rules Committee, kept the bill, H.R. 6400, tied up for more than a month. More complicated than southern resistance was an alternative bill offered by Representative William McCulloch (R-OH). McCulloch was seen by most as the strongest Republican advocate of civil rights in the House. He felt that the Johnson bill was too punitive towards the South while, at the same time, its limited focus on the South did not cover all the areas in the country where blacks were discriminated against and disenfranchised. His bill proposed that federal intervention occur when there were twenty-five "meritorious complaints" of discrimination; the Johnson bill triggered intervention only in those counties where the less than half of the local adults had voted in 1964 and where literacy tests were still used. Because it placed the burden of proof back on the victims, a number of Republicans and many southerners supported the McCulloch bill. However, most members saw through this weakening effort and the Johnson-supported version of the bill was passed.

In the joint Senate-House conference to work out the differences in the bill, some important compromises were made. The conference threw out a provision in the House version of the bill that would have eliminated the poll tax in state and local elections. Although the Twenty-fourth Amendment had rejected poll taxes in federal elections, they continued to be used in other elections. In a concession to pass the bill, King sent word that he would not challenge that decision by the conference. Also, under the sponsorship of freshman Senator Robert Kennedy (D-NY), a provision was added that made it easier for Puerto Ricans to register and vote.

August 6
On August 3, the House passed the conference bill 328 to 74 and the Senate passed the billion August 4.[12] On

August 6, in an elaborate White House ceremony in the President's Room, Johnson signed the bill into law. Ironically, this was the same date and in the same room where Lincoln had signed the Emancipation Proclamation. Johnson stated, "Today is a triumph for freedom as huge as any victory that has ever been won on any battlefield."[13]

THE IMPACT OF THE VRA

At the signing of the legislation, Johnson stated, "I pledge we will not delay or we will not hesitate, or will not turn aside until Americans of every race and color and origin in this country have the same rights as all others to share in the progress of democracy."[14] Within days of the signing, counties all over the South were designated to receive federal examiners and within a few months thousands of blacks had become new registrants.

Between 1964 and 1969, in every southern state the number of registered blacks rose sharply and, in some instances, tripled or quadrupled.

Prior to 1965, there had been no blacks elected to Congress from the South since the end of the nineteenth century. In 1965 in the South, there were only 72 black elected officials in the entire region.[15] Within a few years of the passage of the Voting Reform Act, a significant increase in black elected officials at all levels became evident. In 1972, Andrew Young (D-GA) and Barbara Jordan (D-TX) were elected to Congress. The real growth, however, occurred at the state level.[16]

Many civil rights activists believe the Voting Rights Act is the most important single piece of legislation in U.S. history in the service of democracy. The Act was extended in 1970, and important revisions were made to the bill in 1975 and 1985.

Ambassador Andrew Young

BLACK ELECTED OFFICIALS OUTSIDE THE SOUTH

Scholar Robert Smith argues that, in addition to the VRA and other civil rights gains, there were other critical factors that influenced the increase in black elected officials including: the rise of the black power movement, the expansion of the black middle-class, black involvement in government antipoverty programs which expanded the number of blacks who gained experience in how government functions, growth in the black population in urban areas, and ghetto rebellions.[17]

Black Power

The black power era was symbolically kicked-off on June 16, 1966, during a civil rights march in Mississippi, when activists from the Student Non-violent Coordinating Committee (SNCC), Stokely Carmichael and Willie Ricks, began to use the chant "Black Power." Though the term had been used in the past by others, the media picked up on the term and a resurgent black nationalist movement under the banner cry of black power quickly swept across the country. On July 17, 1967, the first national black power conference was held in Newark.

The black power politics in the late sixties and early seventies swept up even conservative blacks who interpreted it as a call for inclusion. Republican senator Edward Brooke, for example, stated, "I am not an advocate of black power in the sense that the term has come to mean violence. But power as the ability to change conditions so that opportunities are opened, right [sic] respected and enforced, and a man's future made secure, is the essence of the democratic process. The poor, especially the Negro poor, must become full participants in that process."[18]

The growth in black militance coincided with the

Senator Edward Brooke

growth of the black middle-class due to opportunities in government and to the doors opened by the civil rights movement.

Just as the period between World War I and World War II had seen great migrations of blacks out of the South and out of rural areas, this pattern was repeated, to a lesser degree, in the 1960s. In most major cities, the black population grew. (See Table). This increase was also due to the flight of whites to the suburbs during this time. As the number of blacks grew as a percentage of the population, the ability to elect blacks to office was realized. In nearly all of these cities, an African American would be elected to office between 1965 and 1975.

A final and critical factor was the ghetto rebellions of the time and the black and white response to them. Between 1965 and 1968, in New York City, Detroit, Newark, and dozens of other cities, ghettos erupted in violent revolt as poor and working class blacks reacted to instances of police brutality or, in 1968, the assassination of Martin Luther King, Jr. Following these uprisings, many blacks felt that it was imperative that blacks hold political office.

In 1967, civil rights attorney Thurgood Marshall was appointed to the Supreme Court by President Lyndon Johnson while Senator Edward Brooke (R-MA) began the first of his two terms in the U.S. Senate. There were a lot of "firsts" at this time. Robert C. Weaver, Johnson's secretary of Housing and Urban Development was the first black cabinet member; Andrew Brimmer was the first black governor of the Federal Reserve Board; and Patricia Harris became the first black woman ambassador upon her appointment to Luxembourg.[19]

The numbers of black women elected grew steadily over the years. From articulate and influential congresswomen, such as Barbara Jordan (D-TX) and Shirley Chisholm (D-NY), to women who served as mayors, state officials, and school board members, black women legislators have been an integral part of black political leadership though were not always accepted as such. In 1970 there were 160 black female elected officials; in 1993, there were 2,332.

The growth in black elected officials has led to the development of a number of new organizations: the Congressional Black Caucus, the National Conference of Black Mayors, the National Black Caucus of Local Elected Officials, National Black Caucus of State Legislatures, and the National Black Women's Political Leadership Caucus. All of these groups have attempted to take advantage of the rise in numbers and influence that black elected officials have achieved in the thirty years since the passage of the Voting Rights Act.

CHAPTER SEVEN

The Congressional Black Caucus

In the political confusion following the 1968 assassination of Martin Luther King, Jr., and the "crisis of victory" that affected the movement, groups advocating social revolution, such as the Black Panthers and the Revolutionary Action Movement had momentarily eclipsed the civil rights movement. At the same time, others began to promote a strategy of massive black voter registration, voter turnout, and electing blacks to public office. Against this backdrop, the Congressional Black Caucus was formed.

THE EARLY YEARS

By 1969 black members formed the Democratic Select Committee (DSC). It had no staff, no budget, and no officers except Representative Charles Diggs (D-MI), who was elected chairman by consensus.

The DSC was instrumental in founding the Joint Center for Political Studies, the African American think tank that provides to black legislators in Congress policy research and analysis related to black interests. It continues to exist today, renamed the Joint Center for Political and Economic Studies.

As the number of black representatives grew, some pleaded for more organization. On New Year's Eve 1970, Representative William Clay (D-MO) wrote a proposal that stated "without adequate programming and planning, we might as well degenerate into the Kongressional Koffee Klatch Club."[1]

The name Democratic Select Committee clearly linked the group to the Democratic Party, which some members viewed as problematic. In fact, the only black Republican member of Congress at the time, Senator Edward Brooke (R-MA), refused to join the group during his two terms in the Senate (1967–1979), because he considered it to be essentially a Democratic Party organization. The group finally settled on Congressional Black Caucus and was officially launched in 1971 when by that time their number had grown to twelve. "Black people have no permanent friends, no permanent enemies, just permanent interests," became the official motto of the Congressional Black Caucus.[2]

One of the first activities of the CBC was to respond to a rebuf—Nixon's rejection of a February 1970 request for a meeting by black members in the House of Representatives. Representative Louis Stokes (D-OH), recognizing the need for some type of dramatic action, suggested that the black members boycott Nixon's 1971 State of the Union address. The boycott was carried out by all of the black members with the exception of Senatpr Brooke. The impact of the protest, and support by some Republicans, forced Nixon to announce that he would meet with the CBC on March 25, 1971.

To prepare for the meeting, the CBC solicited dozens of black intellectuals and activists around the nation to submit suggestions on how to improve the situation of African Americans. This included some of the best known black leaders at the time including the NAACP's Roy Wilkins, the Urban League's Whitney Young, and the A. Phillip Randolph Institute's Bayard Rustin. About four hundred position papers were submitted and eventually sixty specific recommendations were created to be presented to Nixon. Among the recommendations were requests for the creation of 1.1 million public service jobs, investigation of voting rights violations, release of eight hundred million dollars for domestic programs, release of one hundred fifty million dollars in low-income housing funds, a swift end to the Vietnam War, establishment of a civil rights division in the Department of Defense, and a serious effort to address the problem of drug trafficking and addiction.[3] The CBC asked that Nixon respond within two months. When he did respond, on May 18, Nixon mainly reported on the programs that his administration was already doing, and he generally ignored many of the demands that had been presented by the CBC.

The 1972 National Black Political Assembly (NBPA) conference, held on March 10–12, was a major effort to bring together the widest array of black activists and black elected officials, from both parties, as well as nationalists, radicals, and others who generally opposed working with the Democrats and Republicans. The controversies that arose during the organizing for the convention and the gathering itself nearly split the CBC.

The CBC did not officially participate in the NBPA. However, Representaive Charles Diggs was one of the three national co-convenors of the NBPA along with Gary, Indiana, mayor Richard Hatcher and radical nationalist leader Amiri Baraka. Walter Fauntroy, the delegate from Washington, D.C., headed up the Platform Committee. Representatives John Conyers (D-MI) and

Ron Dellums (D-CA) were also heavily involved in the activities of the convention.

The alliance of radical activists and elected officials did not last long. Two planks that were passed split the convention into different camps. One resolution condemned the state of Israel, while the other opposed busing. The Israeli resolution stated that "the establishment of the Jewish State of Israel in 1948 constituted a clear violation of the Palestine traditional right to life in their own homeland" and argued that "the historical land of Palestinian and Arab people be returned to them."[4] The busing resolution denounced court-ordered busing, claiming, "busing has officially been used to maintain segregation" in education.[5] Other contentious issues also surfaced at the convention including a debate over calling for an all-black political party and endorsement of the presidential campaign of CBC member Shirley Chisholm (D-NY).

CBC members individually issued statements disavowing the positions taken by the convention and distanced themselves from any of its activities. The CBC itself issued a press statement supporting busing and defending Israel that read, "We pledge our continued support to the concept that Israel has the right to exist in peace as a nation."[6] After this controversy, there was little working relationship between the black elected officials and the nationalist and radical activists.

Meanwhile, divisions were growing over the Chisholm presidential candidacy. Antagonisms grew as many of the black members claimed that Chisholm had never confided her intentions to run to the CBC and that she was being a disruptive force in the plans by black leaders to forge a unified strategy for the 1972 race.

Chisholm and her supporters, on the other hand, noted with some legitimacy that black male leaders were more concerned about cutting deals with the Democratic

Shirley Chisholm

Party than developing a real, progressive agenda. She believed that her being a woman was also a large factor in how she was treated and the failure to support her. For example, the "secret" meetings by black leaders to develop a strategy were virtually all-male affairs. The leaders of this effort were Jesse Jackson, Julian Bond, Percy Sutton, Richard Hatcher, Walter Fauntroy, Willie Brown, Maynard Jackson, Amiri Baraka, Clarence Mitchell III, Basil Patterson, Stokes, Diggs, Conyers, and Rangel.[7] There was not a single woman in the core group. Chisholm did receive endorsements from three black members: Dellums, Conyers, and Parren Mitchell.[8]

In the end, most of the black members and other black leadership endorsed the Democratic nominee, George McGovern. Although he won 85 percent of the black vote, McGovern was crushed in the general election by Richard Nixon. McGovern lost forty-nine of the fifty states in one of the most lopsided losses in U.S. history.[9]

After Nixon's resignation from the presidency following the Watergate scandal in 1974, the CBC hoped that its relations with incoming President Ford would be more productive. This was not to be the case.

In the 1976 presidential contest, most of the black members worked hard for Jimmy Carter. Some worked for Ted Kennedy or other candidates during the primaries, but after Carter won the nomination all the Democratic members rallied behind him. In the general election, Carter lost the majority of white voters, but won more than 90 percent of the black vote, which many believe made him owe his election to the black community.[10]

Carter appointed a large number of blacks to positions in his administration, including Patricia Harris as secretary of Housing and Urban Development, and Andrew Young as ambassador to the United Nations. However, Carter would soon disappoint both the the CBC and the general black community. He initiated few programs for blacks and during the last year of his administration actually began to make cuts in social programs, many of which benefited blacks.

While Carter would be frustrating, CBC relations with his successor, Ronald Reagan, would be worse yet. After one mainly symbolic meeting during his first year in office, Reagan simply refused to meet again with the CBC for the rest of his eight years in office. More important, his administration had little in common with the CBC agenda and it promoted conservative blacks. Although two prominant civil rights activists, Reverend David Abernathy and Hosea Williams, had endorsed Reagan in 1980 out of anger with Carter, the civil rights community would receive nothing but antagonism from the new administration.[11] Reagan even was endorsed by the Invisible Empire of the Ku Klux Klan whose leader, Bill Wilkinson stated "anytime you see all the blacks and minorities in this country opposing, strongly, one man, you know he has got to be doing something good for the white race."[12]

From black members of Congress to big-city mayors, the Reagan era meant trouble for black politicians. Despite a Democratic majority in the U.S. House of Representatives, Reagan was able to pass budgets that made major cuts in social programs supported by the black and civil rights communities. While military spending was increased 46 percent, housing was slashed by 77 percent and education by 70 percent.[13]

Reagan also opposed the Civil Rights Restoration Act and the extension of the Voting Rights Act in 1982. Policy toward South Africa is a good example of the political differences between the CBC and Reagan. Once in office, Reagan announced his administration's policy toward South Africa of "constructive engagement." By this it was meant that there would be little public criticism of apartheid in South Africa. Supposedly, the apartheid regime would be criticized behind closed doors, but few believed that that had ever occurred. In response to the South African government's continuing denial of human and political rights to blacks, Representative Dellums and the CBC proposed and passed legislation—the Anti-Apartheid Act of 1986—that would provide strong economic sanctions against South Africa. Reagan opposed the legislation and vetoed it, forcing Congress to override his veto.

One symbolic victory that the CBC was able to get during the Reagan era was the passage of the Martin Luther King, Jr. Federal Holiday Bill. The bill had been introduced by Representative John Conyers (D-MI) in 1968, shortly after King's assassination. Although he did not support the bill, Reagan was forced to sign it into legislation.[14]

Reagan made what many considered racist statements or engaged in racist behavior. He talked about "welfare queens," laid a wreath at the graves of Nazi soldiers in Germany, did not recognize his only black Cabinet member, Secretary of Housing and Urban Development Sam Pierce, nominated ultra-conservative Robert Bork to the Supreme Court, and in 1983 invaded the tiny Caribbean island of Grenada.[15]

Beginning in 1981, the CBC began to produce an annual "CBC Alternative Budget"—a balanced budget that also paid for needed social programs by progressively taxing the rich and cutting military spending.

CBC unity around its alternative budget began to unravel somewhat in 1985 when Bill Gray (D-PA) became chairman of the House Budget Committee. Now, as a member of the Democratic leadership, Gray's divided loyalties were apparent. While offering rhetorical support for the CBC budget, Gray did not vote for it and worked hard to pass the consensus Democratic leadership version of the budget.

During the Reagan years, the CBC was able to win lit-

Ron Dellums displays paper airplanes made of dollar bills in a protest against allocating money for the B-2 stealth bomber.

tle support for its budget on the House floor. The budget was defeated in 1981 by 356 to 69, and by 1995 even some black members voted against it.

In 1988, although George Bush had promised a "kinder and gentler" America than the one run by Ronald Reagan, very little changed in administration policies regarding black concerns. During the campaign, Bush refused to denounce the infamous "Willie Horton" campaign ads produced by one of his supporters, which promoted stereotype images of black males as perpetual criminals.

Bush's veto of the 1991 Civil Rights Bill, his "war on drugs," and his 1989 invasion of Panama alienated the caucus. Without a doubt, the most brutal battle between Bush and the black community occurred over the Bush nomination of black conservative Clarence Thomas to the Supreme Court. As a Reagan official, Thomas had opposed every goal of the civil rights community. During his tenure as head of the Equal Employment Opportunity Commission, he had refused to vigorously apply the law and been called before Congress on several occasions on the matter. The CBC was one of the first black organizations to announce their opposition to the nomination. Despite their organized resistance, Thomas prevailed.

THE CHAIR

In 1992, for the first time in its history the CBC had a contested race for the chair. Kweisi Mfume (D-MD) served as CBC vice chair in the 102nd Congress and by precedent was set to inherit the chair position. However, Craig Washington announced his intention to buck tradition and become the CBC chair. While some in the media sought to portray the race as a power-grab by Washington, in fact, Mfume and Washington had sharply distinct ideas about the role of the CBC in the 103rd

Kweisi Mfume

Congress and how it should be run. When the battle was over, Kweisi Mfume emerged as the victor to lead the CBC during the 103rd, beating Craig Washington 27 to 9.[16]

Some in the CBC and others felt that under Mfume, there would be very little change in how the CBC functions; for example, the CBC would only move on issues in which there is consensus, an increasingly difficult prospect as the numbers grow. His victory, as one journalist noted, "represented the power of tradition more than any overwhelming mandate."[17] Washington, on the other hand, envisioned a much more activist CBC. Focusing on their difference in style, Washington asked members, "Do you want someone who is willing to ruffle a few feathers and make a few waves when necessary? Or do you want someone who is more consensus-oriented?"[18] Arriving from Texas in 1989, filling the seat held by the late Mickey Leland, Craig Washington developed a detailed program of action that he had hoped to implement if he had won.

In 1994, another contested race for the leadership of the CBC emerged in the battle between Donald Payne (D-NJ) and Alcee Hastings (D-FL). Payne was the eventual winner as the older members voted for him (and the CBC seniority system), while some of the newer members voted for Hastings. This election took place in the context of the victorious Republican majority threatening to eliminate the Legislative Service Organizations (LSOs), the House-funded internal organizations, including the CBC. Authorized LSOs were funded through dues paid out of congressional members' official office budgets and were allowed to use office space, the House mail service, and congressional equipment. Dues ranged from five thousand dollars to as much as ten thousand dollars depending upon the group. While several Republican-oriented and dominated LSOs, such as the Republican

Study Committee and the House Wednesday Group, were also disposed of in the sweep, most believe that the real targets were liberal groups like the CBC and the research-oriented Democratic Study Group. As the majority party, the Republicans had and used their authority to abolish the LSOs.

While members still had the right to meet as often as they liked, it would be without a separate staff, budget, equipment, or office space. In any case, unless the Democrats regain control of the House of Representatives, Democratic black members will find little receptivity to their policy agenda. They will remain a minority within a minority with no power to shape the political direction of Congress via the legislative process. However, even in this situation, similar to the role that the few blacks in Congress played at the end of the last century, African American members can remain a voice for the poor, dispossessed, and others who remain locked out of the mainstream of society. The challenge facing black members is to have their concerns heard, which may require a level of activism and the development of new strategies never seen before within and without the halls of Congress.

BLACK MEMBERS OF CONGRESS IN THE 1990s

In the 1990s, black members of Congress have reached a new stage of development. The election of a Democratic president Bill Clinton in 1992, the Republican takeover of both chambers of Congress in 1994, the status of being a minority within a minority in the House of Representatives, and the official decrease of the authority of the Congressional Black Caucus by the Republican-controlled Congress in 1995 complicate profoundly the political tasks of black members. Under the leadership of

Newt Gingrich (R-GA), the CBC and other similar groups inside of Congress had their offices taken away, their budgets and staff completely cut, and their status reduced to that of essentially a volunteer association. Although to a great degree the perceived power of the CBC was always greater than its real power, the change in power in Congress is a serious blow to the legislative and political aspirations of black members.

These challenges emerge at a time when political and ideological diversity within the CBC is the greatest, ranging from the extreme conservatism of Republican Representatives Gary Franks and J. C. Watts to the "socialist" orientations of Representatives John Conyers and Ronald Dellums and many shades in between.

In 1995, the forty-one black members of Congress included forty members in the U.S. House of Representatives and one member, Carol Moseley-Braun, in the U.S. Senate. Braun is the fourth African American, the only African American Democrat, and the only African American woman ever to serve in the U.S. Senate.[19] In the U.S. House of Representatives, there were thirty-seven Democrats and two Republicans, and one Independent. Of the forty blacks in the House, thirty-eight are full representatives and two, Eleanor Holmes Norton (D-DC) and Vincent Frazer (I-VI), are delegates who have no voting rights on the House floor.[20]

African American members represent about 20 percent of the House of Representatives Democratic membership and about 9 percent of the overall membership in the House. When the Democrats controlled the House of Representatives these figures meant that the CBC could easily be the margin of decision on many votes. In addition, in the 103rd Congress (1993–1994), black members chaired three full committees and seventeen subcommittees. African American members are also distributed throughout the leadership bodies of the House.

As a result of the 1992 congressional elections, when a record number of new black members were added to the thirty-six that were already in Congress, black membership became more rural, southern, and female than in previous years. At least one-third of the African American members have significant rural populations in their districts, particularly most of the relatively new members from the South, such as Georgia's Cynthia McKinney and Alabama's Earl Hillard. As of 1995, seventeen of the forty-one members were from the South, representing forty-one percent of the black representatives.

Gender balance among blacks in Congress has also changed in the last fifteen years. In 1979, two African American women were in the seventeen-member African American delegation of the 96th Congress (12 percent). In contrast, there are twelve African American women in the 104th Congress, constituting about 29 percent of the black members.

Similar to earlier periods, black members are highly educated, held high-status positions before they arrived in Congress, and, in general, had incomes higher than that of the average African American. While two members do not have college degrees, thirty-eight members are at least college graduates with more than half of those holding advanced degrees. Sixteen have law degrees, ten have Master's degrees or MBAs, and one is a doctoral candidate.[21]

Perhaps the most dramatic development in recent times was the level of participation by African American members in the leadership bodies and structures of Congress. Prior to the Republican victories, John Lewis was a deputy whip while Bobby Rush (D-IL) won one of the three whip positions open to new members.

The Democratic Congressional Campaign Committee (DCCC) is another critical source of power within the House Democratic structure. It is the body that doles out

Cynthia McKinney

campaign funds. Since its budget is limited, hard decisions must be made about which Democratic campaigns are to be financially supported and which candidates are to be left to fend for themselves. The African American members of the DCCC are John Lewis, Maxine Waters, Bill Jefferson, Kweisi Mfume, Craig Washington, and Eleanor Holmes Norton.

All of the African American members that came to Congress in 1993 brought with them many years of legislative and municipal experience with the exception of Representative Mel Reynolds (D-IL), who never held elected office until his congressional victory. In this sense, they are different from the wave of African American members who came in during the late 1960s and early 1970s. Many, if not most, of those earlier members came out of the civil rights community, the church, or political activism. They had little or no legislative experience. Among the new African American faces taking office in 1993 were eight who were state senators, three who were in state Houses, one former mayor, one former alderman, one former U.S. district judge, and two who were longtime appointed government officials.

New members also brought other differences. Given the partially rural nature of the districts of many of the new members, the African American members' priorities were affected dramatically. For instance, the Caucus will no longer enjoy unanimous consent on massive aid to urban cities, which characterizes the districts of most of the old members, if there is no equal funding for rural areas. Representative Cynthia McKinney is representative of this new perspective. She states, "Until now southern black people, rural black people, have been totally left out of Congress and the Black Caucus. I've got people in my district with no running water, people fighting for the right to vote . . . 30 percent of my district is white."[22] She is like many of the new members who come from congres-

Above: Bobby Rush in black hat as chairman of the Illinois Black Panthers following Fred Hampton's murder by Chicago police. Below: Representative Bobby Rush of Illinois with House Speaker Tom Foley

sional districts that have large rural and large white tracts.

While their previous legislative experience makes them better able to negotiate Congress than their predecessors, that same experience also has a tendency to make the new African American members more system-oriented and less willing to challenge the status quo outside of the bounds of congressional decorum and moderation.

CHAPTER EIGHT

The 1980s and the Quest for the White House

Although the presidential candidacy of Jesse Jackson in 1984 (and again in 1988) electrified the nation, Jackson was not the first black to seek that office. Since 1856, blacks have been nominated for the offices of president and vice president on both major and minor party tickets. (See Appendix—Black Presidential Candidates.)

PRELUDE TO JACKSON — THE CHICAGO MAYORAL RACE

The Reagan victory of 1980 was viewed as a defeat by many in the black community. Reagan had campaigned on a hardline conservative platform threatening to cut social programs, increase the military budget, and rollback the gains of the civil rights movement. And, within a very short time of being in office, Reagan kept his promises. The Republicans were also able to win the Senate in 1980, holding it for six years and becoming another obstacle to black advance.

Blacks were also frustrated with the Democrats whose votes in Congress helped Reagan to pass his legislative agenda. As a result, African Americans entered the 1983 mayoral races in Chicago (Harold Washington) and in Boston (Mel King); and in 1984 Jesse Jackson campaigned for the Democratic presidential nomination.

A black mayor in Boston or Chicago seemed an unlikely prospect given the strong white ethnic populations and the long histories of racial conflicts in the two cities. Yet, many black activists believed that running a black candidate on a progressive platform could forge enough unity among groups of African Americans, Latinos, women, labor and working classes, and educated whites to form a winning coalition. In Boston, using this strategy, former state assemblyman and community activist Mel King unsuccessfully challenged Raymond Flynn for the mayor's seat. Although he lost in a close race, falling four hundred votes shorts,[1] King ran on a progressive platform that called for a "rainbow coalition" of support from blacks, whites, and Latinos of all backgrounds.

The mayoral race that would rivet the nation, however, occurred in Chicago. By 1982, following what many blacks felt was a disastrous administration by then-mayor Jane Byrne, a number of black leaders felt it was time that an African American be elected mayor. Groups formed for this purpose included the Chicago Black United Communities (CBUC); Citizens for Self-Determination, a local chapter of the National Black United Front (NBUF); and People Organized for Welfare and Economic Reform (POWER) among others. Older organizations, such as Jesse Jackson's Operation PUSH, were also involved. Activists in the black community asked Representative Harold Washington (D-IL) to run for the seat and took on the responsibility of raising several hundred thousand dollars and registering 180,000 new black voters by November 1982.[2]

Mel King

While other candidates had been discussed, including Jesse Jackson, it was thought that Washington was best known and had the best chance of winning in a three-way primary race against Byrne and Richard Daley, Jr., son of former mayor, the legendary Richard Daley. It was a brutal campaign marked with many racist remarks and incidents. Although Washington made a grand effort to build a broad coalition of support from blacks, whites, Latinos, business, the poor, and the wealthy, the resistance to the possibility of an African American controlling city hall brought out the worst in many. Reportedly, some of Byrne's campaign workers distributed leaflets that warned if Washington was elected that Jesse Jackson would actually be running the city.[3] Local Democratic Party chairman Edward Vrdolyak, a perpetual enemy of Washington and supporter of Byrne, appealed to white voters, warning that "a vote for Daley is a vote for Washington. It's a racial thing. Don't kid yourself. I'm calling on you to save your precinct. We're fighting to keep the city the way it is."[4] Vrdolyak knew that Daley's candidacy would take votes away from Byrne. The black community was also angered by the outside support that Byrne and Daley got from national Democratics. Ted Kennedy (D-MA), for example, endorsed Byrne, while Walter Mondale, a candidate for the Democratic nomination, endorsed Daley.

Washington had strong black community support overall; nevertheless, there were some blacks tied to the old Democratic machine who endorsed other candidates. In the end, however, Washington prevailed in a close primary race. He won 36.3 percent of the vote (419,266) to Byrne's 33.4 percent (386,456) and Daley's 29.9 percent (343,506). Washington won easily in the black wards while Byrne won the wealthy white northwest and north sides of the city and Daley won the white ethnic groups (Polish, Irish, and German) on the southwest. Black

Harold Washington, Mayor of Chicago

turnout at 64.2 percent nearly doubled that of only four years earlier at 34.5 percent.[5]

Although Chicago is notorious for its Democratic Party dominance (winning the Democratic primary is tantamount to victory), Washington's general election battle was far from smooth. He faced the little known Republican challenger Bernard Epton who would benefit from the local Democratic Party's antagonism toward Washington. Byrne at first appeared to graciously accept defeat; then in a reversal that was viewed by many as racist sour grapes, she declared that she was going to do a write-in campaign. This effort fizzled fairly quickly and she gave up the attempt. The rest of the old-line Democratic machine continued to work to undermine the Washington campaign. A number of Democrats openly endorsed Epton, including city council chairman Vito Marzullo, aldermen Anthony Laurino, Richard Clewis, Aloysisu Majerczyk, Ivan Rittenberg, and Chicago Park District superintendent Edmund Kelly.[6]

Epton's campaign, in overt and covert ways, exploited the racial conflict existing in the city. His slogan, "Vote Bernard Epton Before It's Too Late," was interpreted by most to mean that a black mayor would be bad news for whites. Other flyers that came out in support of Epton (and which some claimed were distributed by Epton campaign workers) were more overtly racist. Among the warnings were that "white women will be raped," "property values will decline," and the police department would be renamed the "Chicongo Po-lease."[7]

In the end, Washington barely managed to squeak out a victory. In the overwhelmingly Democratic city, he won 50.1 percent (668,176) of the vote to Epton's 46.4 percent (619,926). The racial bloc voting was stunning. Of Epton's total vote, 95 percent came from whites.[8] On the other hand, it was estimated that Washington won close to 98 percent of the black vote.[9]

Jesse Jackson

His first term, while contentious, had made great strides nevertheless. The patronage system was largely dismantled and blacks, Latinos, and others were able to obtain influential jobs at city hall. While Washington fought the twenty-nine (out of fifty) aldermen who sided with his arch-enemy Vrdolyak, his support in the community and throughout the city grew.

In his second bid, in 1987, Washington was easily returned to office. The city council also became much friendlier following the defeat of several Vrdolyak allies. Unfortunately for the city, blacks, and progressives around the nation, Washington's term was cut short when he died of a heart attack on November 26, 1987. Shortly thereafter, the already unstable Washington coalition unraveled as personal ambitions, class differences, and political differences came to the fore. Corporate power was still in control and, despite the progressive agenda articulated by Washington, little had changed in the material life of most blacks in the city. Many of the same issues—symbolism versus substantive benefits— would be manifested at the national level in the 1984 Jesse Jackson campaign for the Democratic presidential nomination.

JACKSON JUMPS IN

Jackson's interest in running for president dates to at least May 1971. At a meeting of Chicago political leaders, Jackson stated, "We're going to talk about a black candidate for President."[10] He went on to say, "Young people and women have a real interest in a black candidate for President."[11] He had also raised the issue during and after the National Black Political Agenda convention in 1972. Jackson not only thought that a black presidential candidate was needed, but perhaps even a black third party. He stated at the convention, "Without the option of a black political party, we are doomed to remain in the hip pocket of the Democratic party and the rumble seat of the Republican party."[12]

By early 1982, with Reagan firmly in the White House, black leaders' backs were up against the wall. In late 1982 and early 1983, black leaders held a series of meetings to discuss strategies for the upcoming 1984 presidential campaign and at one of the meetings, the suggestion was raised of running an African American for the Democratic nomination to put pressure on the Democrats. No consensus was reached on either the strategy or who would possibly be the candidate. In Chicago, on June 20, 1983, the group known as the "black leadership family" endorsed the idea of a black candidate though no specific person was named.[13] Some black leaders, such as Detroit mayor Coleman Young, NAACP executive director Benjamin Hooks, and National Urban League president John Jacobs, opposed the idea.[14] Among those who could possibily be considered were Atlanta mayor Andy Young and various members of the Congressional Black Caucus. Jesse Jackson's name also was mentioned.

Perhaps the best known, if not the best liked, of the black leaders involved in these discussions, Jackson brought both immense strengths and well-known weaknessess to the table. Unlike most black elected officials or civil rights leaders, whose popularity was limited to either the South or their elected constituency, Jackson had a base and reputation around the country. From his southern activist days with Martin Luther King, Jr., to his militant activities in Chicago as head of Operation PUSH, Jackson had been involved in countless battles in many circumstances for more than two decades. Also, unlike many black leaders, while his strength had been his black community fights, he had been engaged in struggles ranging from peace issues and workers' rights to women's concerns and environmental safety. As a minister, he had ties to the national black church network that would be critical in raising funds for his campaign.

Jackson's oratory skills were also important. Well known for his allegorical, rhyming rhetorical style, his capacity to translate complex political ideas into familiar and insightful terms was a necessary skill, given the base of potential voters that he would be seeking to ignite. Trained in the dynamic speaking manner of the black ministry, the most powerful and elegant rhetorical style that exists in the United States, he has persuaded millions to listen to his message. His insurgent approach would be the catalyst that would transform an election campaign into a modern movement of the poor and dispossessed.

Despite these strengths, many were wary of Jackson. Known as a maverick who had difficulty sharing leadership, many of the veterans in the civil rights movement and a large number of black elected officials hesitated to support Jackson's potential candidacy. Some of the civil rights leaders considered Jackson to be overly ambitious, citing the oft repeated story that when Martin Luther King, Jr., was assassinated, Jackson wiped blood from the banister on his shirt and later falsely told the media that he had held King in his arms when he died. That incident along with others made many hesitant to endorse a Jackson candidacy.

Also, many of the black leaders, despite their blustering about being independent, were already making commitments to various whites who were running or about to run for the Democratic nomination. Most of the civil rights leaders, including Coretta Scott King, NAACP's Benjamin Hooks, and Southern Christian Leadership Conference's Joseph Lowery, were already supporting Walter Mondale. Some civil rights leaders, such as Mary Frances Berry of the U.S. Civil Rights Commission and

Carl Holman of the National Urban Coalition, did endorse Jackson.

While these political maneuverings were unfolding in the spring of 1983, the momentum behind a Jackson candidacy was growing. By August, when the massive twentieth anniversary of the 1963 March on Washington was held, it had become clear that if there was going to be a black candidate, it would be Jackson. The most significant occurrence at the march and rally, dubbed "Jobs, Peace and Freedom," was the cry "Run, Jesse, Run" shouted by tens of thousands of the estimated three hundred thousand present.[15] Two months later on November 3, in Washington, D.C., Jackson made his announcement.

Standing before a packed crowd at Washington's Convention Center and sensing the historic moment, Jackson stated,[16]

"I seek the Presidency because I want to affirm my belief that leadership is colorless and genderless, and that the sole hallmark of a true leaders is not the skin color he or she received from God, but the ability of the person to bring competence, compassion and fairness to the sacred trust that the people elect their officials to discharge. . . .

This day we gather strangely exuberant and hopeful amidst so much chaos, confusion, despair, and pain. We sense that we are part of a special moment in history, pregnant with possibility. We courageously press forward for we dare not abort this moment. We are destined to redirect the course of this nation and we shall. We have been hoping against hope, on this journey from slaveship to championships, that the stars in their courses have directed us to this station today.[17]

With some humility, Jackson also spoke of his personal feelings about the path that he was about to seek and perhaps to the past criticism of his political and personal behavior. He reflected,

"I embark upon this course with a sense of inner confidence. I offer myself to the American people, not as a perfect servant, but as a public servant. I offer myself and my service as a vehicle to give a voice to the voiceless, representation to the unrepresented, and hope to the downtrodden."[18]

Finally, Jackson made it clear that he was not just running as a black protest candidate nor that his campaign would only address black concerns. Simultaneously launching his Rainbow Coalition movement, Jackson emphasized,

"Lest there be confusion, let the word go forth from this occasion that this candidacy is not for blacks only. This is a national campaign growing out of the black experience and seen through the eyes of a black perspective—which is the experience and perspective of the rejected. Because of this experience, I can empathize with the plight of Appalachia because I have known poverty. I know the pain of anti-Semitism because I have felt the humiliation of discrimination. . . . I would like to use this candidacy to help build a new rainbow coalition of the rejected that will include whites, blacks, Hispanics, Indian and Native Americans, Asians, women, young people, poor people, old people, gay people, laborers, small farmers, small businesspersons, peace activists, and environmentalists."[19]

Almost overnight, the Jackson campaign turned into a grassroots movement both inside and outside the black community. From students to trade unionists, activists viewed the Jackson campaign as the vehicle through which their concerns could be heard. Jackson was able to forcefully bring into the campaign a wide range of issues that usually went ignored, including ending apartheid in South Africa, nuclear disarmament, aid to the poor, support for labor unions, endorsement of the Equal Rights Amendment, and support for the Palestine cause.

Jackson also sought to fight what he and the campaign viewed as discrimination and undemocratic practices within the Democratic Party. For instance, the party had a winner-take-all rule that meant no matter how well Jackson (or any other candidate) did in a particular state during the primaries, unless you were the winner, you received no delegates. Jackson called for proportional distribution of delegates where any candidate that won at least 15 percent would be allotted delegates based on the percentage of votes they received.

Although Jackson ran a vigorous and spirited campaign, his various primary results fell far short of winning. Resistance from the Democratic Party, reluctance on the parts of whites to vote for a black candidate (even a progressive one that spoke to their issues), divisions among black elected officials and civil rights leaders over supporting Jackson, and severely restricted resources were all factors that contributed to limiting Jackson's important, though modest, victories. Jackson won 3.3 million votes, 61 congressional districts, and 384 convention delegates. Walter Mondale, his main opponent, won 1,635 delegates and the nomination. It should be noted that Jackson argued that the delegate selection process was profoundly unfair.[20]

Jackson's speech at the 1984 Democratic National Convention was a triumphant moment not only for Jackson, but all of black America. Although Jackson had lost the nomination and won few concessions from the party, his presence was proof of the long path that blacks had traveled from the rejection of Fannie Lou Hamer in 1964 to Jackson's delivery of one of the major addresses to the nation. In passage after passage, with passion and verve, Jackson told the story of how blacks and others had come to prevail against the odds in attempting to be part of the democratic system. Acknowledging the gains, Jackson made it clear that the struggle was not over and that black participation would be fought for at every level of politics.

There were other benefits to the Jackson campaign. Jackson and the campaign registered thousands of voters. Many believe that those new voters were responsible for the Democrats winning back the U.S. Senate in 1986, because of the new southern senators that were elected from states with large and now newly registered black populations. These same senators provided the margin of victory in the effort to defeat Reagan Supreme Court nominee Robert Bork in 1987, an arch-conservative who many felt would set back the cause of civil rights.

Jackson also inspired other African Americans to run in local and congressional races. Campaign activist Mabel Thomas, for example, who had never been active politically until the Jackson campaign, ran for the Georgia state House and won. Other than the Jackson campaign, this was her only political experience. In Louisiana, Cleo Fields, a Jackson activist only in his twenties, would be elected to Congress in 1992 after stints in state political offices.

Jackson was also successful in changing the winner-take-all rules although too late for his 1984 campaign. The Democratic National Convention agreed to drop the threshold from 20 percent to 15 percent and limit the number of super-delegates, for example, those delegates who were appointed by party officials.

Jackson ran again in 1988. While his second campaign was much more traditional and his politics were considered slightly more moderate, he was able to broaden his base and remain a player in the game a much longer time than most of the whites running for the office.

Jackson won the following: South Carolina, Alabama, Georgia, Louisiana, Mississippi, Virginia, Arkansas, Puerto Rico, Michigan, Delaware, Washington, D.C., and the Virgin Islands, ninety-two congressional districts, and 6.7 million votes. He finished second in thirty-three states. Some of Jackson's biggest victories came on Super Tuesday (March 8), the day in the campaign when twenty primaries and caucuses were held, mainly in the South where Jackson's base was strongest. He won five states and more than 2.5 million votes that day—more than any other candidate running—and, unlike the others, won delegates from every state. He came in first or second in sixteen of the twenty states.[21]

Jackson's campaigns were an expression, to some degree, of what political scientists call a "leverage" strategy. Although few believed that Jackson could ever win, given the strength of racial prejudice in the United States, it was argued that by building a strong and mobilized base of voters, Jackson and his allies could pressure the Democratic Party to address its concerns. If the Democrats refused to make concessions, then Jackson could theoretically signal his base of voters to withhold their votes from the Democratic Party. This leverage can come from either inside one of the parties ("dependent leverage") or outside of the major party structures ("independent leverage"). Jackson's presidential campaigns are an example of the former, while the mobilization started by H. Ross Perot is an example of the latter.

This strategy has several potential flaws. Jackson and his base must be willing to truly punish the Democrats should their demands be rejected. But the Democrats know that Jackson cannot turn to the Republicans and that Jackson's base has few options. As he discovered in

1992, the Democrats were willing to gamble that they could ignore the demands of the black community or of Jackson himself and still win the election. Given the choice between political moderate Bill Clinton and President George Bush, whose record was considered almost as bad as his predecessor Ronald Reagan, it was not a bad gamble.

AFRICAN AMERICAN CANDIDATES IN 1992

Although Jackson did not enter the 1992 contest, there were two black candidates for president—Ron Daniels and Lenora Fulani—and one for vice president, James Bevel. All three of these candidates ran outside of the two major parties and had little success. Daniels, who ran as an independent, is best known for his work with the National Black Political Assembly and the effort to build the National Black Independent Political Party. Daniels had also been a deputy campaign manager for Jackson in 1988. In the end, Daniels won 25,404 votes.[22]

Fulani's effort was her second run for president under the banner of the controversial New Alliance Party. Fulani stood out in 1992 for several reasons. First, she was able to raise a phenomenal amount of money for a non–major party candidate. Adept at winning matching federal funds, by January 1992 Fulani had raised more than six hundred thousand dollars more than Clinton and most of the Democratic candidates at that time.[23]

One of the surprising candidacies of 1992 was Bevel's run as the vice presidential nominee on the ticket with conservative Lyndon Larouche, well known for his outlandish political conspiracy theories. Larouche was also known for having associations and alliances with members of the Ku Klux Klan, the American Nazi Party, and the leaders of the former apartheid regime in South

Africa. Bevel, on the other hand, had been one of Martin Luther King, Jr.'s key strategists during the civil rights era. He had been central to most of the major battles of that time. However, after King's death, Bevel claimed that the FBI had taken over the SCLC and he quit the organization. He disappeared for a while only to resurface with several right-wing religious organizations. His association with Larouche had little success and they managed to win only about twenty-five thousand votes in 1992.[24]

CHAPTER NINE

Black Elected Officials in the 1990s

The future is not what it used to be. For a great deal of the twentieth century, which has been called the U.S. century, the United States has dominated the world militarily, economically, and politically. The legislative and judicial victories of African Americans in the late 1950s and 1960s, the "Second Reconstruction," were unparalleled except for the brief period of the first Reconstruction (1867–1877). Following World War II, the United States had both the bullets with which to militarily dominate the world and, at the same time, the butter with which to appease its own citizens. In these circumstances, the federal government could afford the reforms won by the civil rights movement.

As the new century approaches, there appears to be little butter left as the "welfare state" is being dismantled. The loss of millions of domestic jobs has worsened living standards in the United States and in the black community in particular. The crisis of the black community occurs at the same moment that black elected officials are under attack by the courts, by a resurgent conservative movement that seeks to destroy the gains of the civil rights movement, and by critics within the black community itself.

Black elected officials are at a dangerous crossroads. While frustration with the Democratic Party has grown, at the same time the Republican Party is perceived to be more hostile to the black community than at any time in the party's history. What are the options? African Americans can either remain loyal to the Democratic Party, switch to the Republican Party, start or join a third party, or run as independent candidates.

BLACKS AND THEIR FUTURE IN THE DEMOCRATIC PARTY

The politics of the party have become more conservative since the civil rights victories of the late 1960s. One signal of this shift was the rise of the Democratic Leadership Council (DLC) in the mid-1980s. The DLC was formed by party moderates and conservatives who were concerned that the party was losing its support among middle-class and white voters. For the DLC politicians, the series of Democratic presidential losses in the 1970s and 1980s could be attributed to making too many concessions to organized "special interests" in the party, such as women's groups, trade unions, and black organizations. They argued that the party had to become more conservative for instance, be more vocal on law and order issues and call for cuts in some social programs.

The DLC was officially formed in 1985 and included among its founding members Bill Clinton, Al Gore, Richard Gephardt, and other congressional and state Democratic leaders. While the DLC was and remains overwhelmingly white, it included a few African Americans such as former representatives Bill Gray and Mike Espy, and former Virginia governor Douglas Wilder.

Many black leaders in the party suspect that the DLC was formed to stop the influence and growth of the Jesse Jackson–led progressive wing of the party. Indeed, in a number of the publications and articles written by DLC officials, Jackson and his supporters were attacked directly. The DLC called for a move away from the "special interests" and back to the political "center." They called themselves New Democrats who were politically neither to the left nor right.

In 1992 the DLC achieved its highest success in the election of Clinton and Gore to the White House. During that campaign, there was a concerted effort to distance the New Democrats from Jackson and the liberal and progressive sectors of the party. As a consequence, Jackson had little influence over the nomination process and the party platform, and his role during the general campaign was essentially to get out the black vote for the Democratic ticket.

Many of the racially-coded issues that the Republicans won on in 1994 were first raised by Clinton during his campaign and his first two years in office. It was Clinton who vowed to "end welfare as we know it" while he was running for office and it was Clinton who sought to appear tough on crime and proposed new crime legislation and promised to put at least a hundred thousand more cops on the streets. Clinton also advocated a balanced budget and called for a "middle class" tax cut, yet offered no similar rhetoric for working class and poor people. And it was President Clinton who fought hard and made deals with Republican conservatives to pass the North American Free Trade Agreement (NAFTA) over the severe and strident objections of the entire labor movement and most black organizations.

With the dominance of the New Democrats, Jackson and other liberal and progressive Democrats, black or white, have been pushed out of the debates over which direction the party should go. That debate is taking place between the New Democrats and the even more conservative wing of the party that is hardly distinguishable from conservative Republicans. This situation has led to calls by some for Jackson to break from the Democratic Party altogether and build a third party. It is clear that many blacks feel that the Democratic Party has perhaps permanently shifted away from supporting black concerns. In the coming years the size of the black vote for Democrats may diminish.

BLACKS AND THEIR FUTURE IN THE REPUBLICAN PARTY

In 1961, conservative Republican leader Barry Goldwater stated, "We're not going to get the Negro vote as a block in 1964 or 1968, so we ought to go hunting where the ducks are."[1] Seven years later this proposal translated into Richard Nixon's infamous "southern strategy," to recruit southern whites away from the Democratic Party by exploiting racial issues, for example, hunting where the ducks are.

Nixon and subsequent Republican presidents used racial codes that were understood by all. Nixon's call for "law and order" and Ronald Reagan's tirade against so-called "welfare queens" were not-too-subtle messages that they would go after what whites perceived as a black criminal and parasitic underclass undermining the nation. Not to be outdone, George Bush launched his deadly "war on drugs" in his first year in office that many interpreted as a war on the African American community.[2] These Republican presidents, in the 1970s and 1980s, also cut social programs that were thought to disproportionately benefit African Americans. In the Reagan era, military spending increased by 46 percent while housing was slashed by 77 percent and education by 70 percent.[3] In 1991 alone, while the U.S. was spending $295 billion on the military, its chief economic competitors, Germany and Japan, were spending only $34 billion and $32 billion respectively.[4] Reagan and Bush also placed individuals on the Supreme Court who are widely perceived to be antagonistic to the concerns of the black community. Civil rights and liberal black leaders found little common ground with those administrations and only rarely were able to have meetings with them to voice their grievances.

The strategy of winning whites back to the Republican party has been successful since the mid-1960s as the Republicans have promoted themselves, to a great degree, as the "white man's" party. As a result, in 1994, for the first time in history, the majority of whites in the South voted Republican giving the party not only control of both chambers of Congress, but the majority of governorships and a majority of southern House legislatures.[5] In addition, a number of elected white Democrats switched to the Republican Party at the congressional, state, and local levels. In Congress, in 1995, Senators Ben Nighthorse Campbell and Richard Shelby and several representatives all switched from being Democrats to Republicans. In July 1995, in a mass defection in Texas, twenty-six elected Democrats changed parties. For many in the South, the Democratic Party increasingly is synonymous with black.

The religious right political movement has also emerged as a critical base for the GOP. In the 1994 elections, for example, the religious right constituted about one-third of those who voted and they nearly unanimously supported Republican candidates.[6] The Christian Coalition, in particular, has been critical in mobilizing millions behind the conservative Republican agenda of ending welfare, eliminating abortion, establishing tougher policies on crime, and downsizing the federal government—positions that the black community continued to oppose in large numbers.

The Republican Party has been able to rebuild itself with the aid of the conservative media. The demagogic discourse on talk radio and television, and in the printed press has echoed the policies of the Republican Party with an intolerance and hysteria unheard of in decades. In this political climate, liberalism is considered the extreme left and Ronald Reagan–type policy is considered the political center. Led by people such as Rush Limbaugh, the conservative media helped direct the legitimate anger of white working people away from the nation's economic and political elites and toward liberals and other groups that have been scapegoated historically in U.S. society. Blacks, immigrants, women, gays and lesbians, and others are being targeted as the cause of white suffering.

A number of prominent black Republicans have appeared in the last few years. This includes Supreme Court Justice Clarence Thomas, Representatives J. C. Watts (R-OK) and Gary Franks (R-CT), former Reagan official Alan Keyes, and radio talk show host Armstrong Williams. These individuals have been extremely vocal in attacking the traditional core of civil rights activists and black elected Democratic officials. They have had minimal success, however, and have gained little support in the black community.

THIRD PARTIES AND INDEPENDENCE

There is a long history in the black community of attempting to build an all-black political party or a multiracial third party. Although these efforts have failed in

Gary Franks

the past, they will likely continue. While some studies show that there is some support for a black party, more than likely any attempt by blacks to go outside of the two major parties will focus on building a multiracial political organization.

Some third party efforts are conservative in nature and receive virtually no support from African Americans. Ross Perot's United We Stand, for example, does not have any visible blacks in its leadership or in any of its grassroots efforts. Older right-wing third parties, such as the Right-to-Life and Populist parties, also have never had strong support from blacks.

In the past, efforts to build progressive third parties have inadequately reached out to black political activists leaving the impression that whites would dominate. Thus, many blacks felt that these efforts did not treat the black community any better than did the Democrats or the Republicans. However, inclusion from the beginning will give these groups a better chance of gaining black community support.

This has been the strategy of The New Party (TNP). From its inception in the late 1980s, TNP has tried to recruit African Americans and other people of color into its leadership and as its candidates for public office. Rather than go after statewide or federal offices, it has tried to win at the municipal level with some modest success. In the mid-1990s, there are other third party efforts such as the Campaign for a New Tomorrow and the Labor Party. Black, Latino, and white activists in the National Committee for Independent Political Action are also involved in supporting third party and independent campaigns.

In some instances, blacks have run for office as independents with little success due to the difficulty that independents have in getting on the ballot and in promoting their campaigns. Unless someone has high-name recognition and an independent source of funding, it is hard to compete with the resources and exposure the major parties give to their candidates. It is likely to be even more difficult in the years ahead. Thus, while the options of going third party or independent may satisfy the need not to be exploited by either the Democrats or Republicans, in the present period there appears to be little hope for success beyond winning a symbolic victory. The dilemma of political direction and strategy, unfortunately, occurs at a time when the economic and social deterioration of the black community seems to be escalating.

THE CRISIS OF THE BLACK COMMUNITY

In the 1980s, the United States spent billions of dollars to build military and intelligence resources to fight genocidal wars in the name of anticommunism while badly needed social services, job training programs, and antipoverty initiatives were underfunded, defunded, or never funded at all. Meanwhile, conditions for many working people in the United States, including African Americans, deteriorated rapidly. Blacks would suffer from the changes in the economy that saw high-paying manufacturing jobs leave the country and go to other lands where labor was cheaper. In the past, low-skilled, entry-level employment had been the means out of poverty for many African Americans. Employed at auto and steel factories and shops in Detroit, Chicago, Pittsburgh, Los Angeles and in many other cities and towns, young African American males and their families were able to become economically stable and have confidence that their children would be able to attend school, that housing would be accessible, and that a future was more or less assured.

Those hopes evaporated rapidly during the 1980s as millions of manufacturing jobs were eliminated. In 1981,

20.2 million people worked in manufacturing. A decade later there was a decline resulting in 1.8 million fewer workers. At the same time, the number of people who became sixteen years of age or older and entered the nation's labor pool grew by 19.4 million individuals.[7] These changes disproportionately affected the African American poor and unskilled.

As a consequence, poverty in the black community exploded. Under Reagan and Bush, from 1981 to 1991, more than 1.6 million additional African Americans fell below the poverty line.[8] By the mid-1980s, about half of all African American children lived under the poverty level. The official poverty rate for African Americans is 33.1 percent, more than ten million people—one-third of black America—which is higher than for Hispanics (30.6 percent), Asians (15.3 percent), or whites (12.2 percent).[9] The crisis threatening the African American community is not simply that there is African American poverty; rather it centers around the chronic nature of that poverty.

Even middle-class African Americans find themselves trailing whites when it comes to economic cushions. According to the Urban League, African Americans have fewer savings accounts than whites (44.5 percent vs. 76.6 percent), fewer checking accounts (30.1 percent vs. 50.9 percent), fewer stocks (7 percent vs. 23.9 percent), less equity in their homes (43.5 percent vs. 66.7 percent), and fewer IRAs (6.9 percent vs. 26.4 percent). African American family income is about 54 percent that of whites— where it was thirty years ago—but, the net worth of African American households is $26,130 compared with $111,950 for whites.

Even in a time of economic recession, African Americans fare worse than other groups. According to the *Wall Street Journal,* "Blacks were the only racial group to suffer a net job loss during the 1990-91 economic downturn."[10]

While whites gained 71,144 jobs, Asians 55,104, and Hispanics 60,040, African Americans lost an estimated 59,479. This all occurred while the companies involved were adding over 116,000 jobs in both service and sales, low-end jobs where African Americans have traditionally been concentrated. At companies such as W. R. Grace, BankAmerica, ITT, Sears, Roebuck and Company, Cocacola, Safeway, Campbell Soup Company, Walt Disney, and General Electric, African Americans lost jobs at a rate twice that of whites. Overall, African Americans had worked in one-third of all blue collar jobs lost during the period.

The crisis extends into every social area. African Americans constitute 21.9 percent of the thirty-seven million Americans under sixty-five who have no health care insurance.[11] As one writer noted, major health issues confront African Americans who "die an average five years earlier than whites, are twice as likely to die before their first birthday, [and] have the highest cancer rate of any U.S. group."[12] *USA Today* reports that an *American Journal of Public Health* study, echoing other reports, found that race was a significant factor in the medical health and health care received by people of color.[13]

The infant mortality rate for African American children is higher than for children in thirty-one nations including Cuba and Kuwait.[14] As researcher Chris Booker wrote, "For black males, the disadvantaged heath status is a cradle-to-grave experience."[15] African American male death rates are twice that of white male death rates at nearly every age level. For those aged 5 to 14, African Americans die at a rate of 195 per hundred thousand while for whites it's 145 per hundred thousand. Between the ages 45 to 54, African American male mortality is 1,244 per hundred thousand and for white males, 578 per hundred thousand.[16] Overall, African American male life expectancy (65.4), which fell during the Reagan years, is lower than for white men, white women, and African American women.[17]

African Americans as a whole die at extraordinarily higher rates than whites of the eight major causes. For example, African Americans die of heart disease at a rate 39 percent greater than whites. The numbers are equally alarming for other causes including cirrhosis and other liver disease (7 percent), strokes (82 percent), diabetes (132 percent), cancer (32 percent), accidents (24 percent), kidney failure (176 percent), and homicides and police killings (500 percent).[18] AIDS and HIV-related deaths are increasing as death rates for African American men have grown to be three times that of white men and nine times greater for African American women than for white women.[19]

ELECTIONS THAT CHANGED BLACK POLITICS

In the late 1980s and early 1990s, a number of dramatic campaigns highlighted the importance of black participation in elections. This includes the elections of David Dinkins, who became the first black mayor of New York City; former Virginia Governor Douglas Wilder, who became the first black elected governor in the United States, both in 1989, and the reemergence of former and once-again D.C. mayor Marion Barry, whose reelection in 1994 after leaving office in political disgrace is one of the more remarkable political comebacks.

Because he could be the first black mayor of the nation's largest city, Dinkins's campaign became a grassroots movement in the city's black community. He was also the direct beneficiary of the 1988 Jesse Jackson campaign for the Democratic presidential nomination. Tens of thousands of black, Latino, poor, labor, and working people were registered during the Jackson campaign and

New York City Mayor David Dinkins

*Douglas Wilder, Governor of Virginia (center), with Lt. Governor Don
Beyer (left) and Attorney General Mary Sue Terry*

they became the target group for the successful Dinkins
campaign one year later. Efforts to unite these groups in
the past had failed but in 1989, according to researchers
Gerard Bushell and Jocelyn Sargent, "Racial polarization,
growing economic inequality, and corruption scandals
were catalysts amongst blacks, white liberals, and Latinos

to minimize their political differences."[20] This coalition was able to defeat the coalition of white ethnic groups, many of whom were Democrats, who supported Dinkins's Republican challenger. Dinkins served only one term, going down in defeat in 1993 to Rudolph Guiliani in a close race.

In Virginia, Douglas Wilder, a political moderate, ran a more traditional campaign. He downplayed race and the fact that if he won he would be the first African American elected to governor in the history of the United States. He had already been the state's first black senator and its first black lieutenant governor. In the 1989 governor's race, he won a squeaker over Republican challenger Marshall Coleman by only 6,854 votes—less than half of one percent. This was in a state that traditionally was Democratic. He won only 39 percent of the white vote. Wilder held conservative positions on many issues—support for the death penalty, opposition to statehood for the District of Columbia, and agreement with Virginia's right-to-work laws—yet still found that many whites were reluctant to vote for a black candidate.

One of the most remarkable political phenomena in the black community, indeed, in U.S. history, was the rise, fall, and rise again of Marion Barry, the mayor of Washington, D.C. In 1990, after twelve years as the city's mayor, Barry was arrested in a FBI-police sting operation where he was videotaped smoking crack cocaine and arrested on the spot. The political fallout from that incident led Barry to decide not to seek reelection for mayor that year although, strangely, he did run a losing campaign for city council. He was subsequently convicted on a misdemeanor drug charge, though not one emanating from the sting operation, and served six months in jail.

In 1992, within months of getting out of jail, Barry again ran for city council, and, in a surprise to most, won decisively against the incumbent. Adopting an African name, Anwar Amal, and dressing in flamboyant African garb, Barry built a strong grassroots movement to propel him back into elected office. Barry's comeback was not finished, however.

He entered the 1994 Democratic primary for mayor against the then-hapless current mayor, Sharon Pratt Kelly, and his chief opponent, Councilman John Ray. The movement Barry had built in his home base in Ward 8 spread throughout the city. The disgraced politician who had been declared dead and buried rose Phoenix-like to conquer his opponents. In the end, Barry won 47 percent of the vote to Ray's 37 percent and Kelly's woeful 13 percent. He won six of the city's eight wards while Kelly did not win a single precinct. In the end, it was not Barry's past of womanizing or cocaine use that was decisive, but rather the mobilization of black poor and working class voters who believed that a redemptive Barry best represented their interests. One factor that helped Barry was the increase in the number of working class and poor blacks registered to vote. Registration rolls surged in working class areas of the city, partially due to changes in the law that made registration easier, but also due to aggressive work by the Barry campaign. Voters in poor and working class neighborhoods were able to reach parity with the city's well-to-do as more than fifty thousand new voters were added to the rolls between 1990 and 1994, most in the year before the election.

Barry put together a street operation that included seasoned political workers, but also the homeless, ex-felons, welfare mothers, seniors, service station attendants, and, to Kelly's chagrin and embarrassment, city workers. His remarkable but underappreciated 1992 council victory was the testing ground for his revived machine. By election day 1994, the machine was running with Rolex precision. The Barry campaign had hundreds of taxis and vans picking up people from homeless shelters and senior homes and taking them to vote up until the polls closed. Kelly was never able to overthrow her "elitist" middle-class image while Ray became, as one opponent called him, the "Great White Hope" supported by the city's outnumbered white community.

These three campaigns and hundreds more involving black elected officials were able to mobilize hundreds of thousands of blacks to get involved in electoral politics. Though their supporters may have been disappointed by their performance once in office, they generated campaigns of enthusiasm and hope, if only for a short time.

BLACK ELECTED OFFICIALS IN THE 1990s

The number of black elected officials is at an all-time high. By 1995, there were more than eighty-five hundred black elected officials in the United States.[21] At every level, from mayors to members of Congress, the numbers have increased in the three decades since the passage of the Voting Rights Act. As the second and third generation of modern black elected officials assume power, more political diversity is also emerging and unity among black politicians may be more elusive than ever.

One key factor in the 1990s, however, is that the number of black elected officials may have reached a peak. First, the number of jurisdictions and locales that have a black majority or near majority have been heard from and it has primarily been from these communities that black elected officials have emerged. Given the reluctance of whites to vote for blacks, even in the 1990s, it is still rare that a black is elected in a political jurisdiction where blacks are not the majority.

Second, black elected officials are also under attack from the courts. The Supreme Court and a number of lower courts have been questioning the legality of majority-minority political districts. In the case of *Shaw v. Reno*, a lawsuit brought by whites challenged the constitutionality of a congressional district created by North Carolina, which produced a majority black congressional district that in 1992 elected Melvin Watt, who is African American. The Supreme Court concluded that the district's "bizarre" shape existed solely because of race and, therefore, was unconstitutional. In 1995, the Supreme Court ruled in *Miller v. Johnson* that a congressional district in Georgia was unconstitutional because it used "race" as the chief factor in determining how the district would look. Other cases, from Louisiana to Florida to Texas, involving the constitutionality of congressional districts that had been drawn to create a black majority voting population, were also being scrutinized by the Supreme Court. Elaine Jones, director of the NAACP Legal Defense Fund, stated that "the districts of virtually every member of the Congressional Black Caucus would be in jeopardy" if the Supreme Court rules against the already established majority black districts.[22]

There are other variables in this period. Some African Americans who are elected in majority white districts have run campaigns where they consciously choose to minimize the race issue. These candidates have been called "post-black" or "deracialized"; for example, they attempt to move away from issues that highlight their race. In some instances, liberal and radical blacks, such as Representative Ron Dellums (D-CA), have been elected in nonblack districts by appealing to whites and Latinos as well as the black community. These politicians have not run away from race, but incorporated it into their broader political appeal. In other instances, some moderate and conservative blacks have been openly hostile to a black or civil rights agenda and have been elected to office by a majority of whites. Gary Franks (R-CT) and J. C. Watts (R-OK), both of whom are African American, were elected to Congress as conservative Republicans who opposed nearly all of the propositions of the civil rights movement.

Despite these factors, it is highly unlikely that black politicians will abandon the Democratic Party at this juncture. More than 90 percent of all current black elected officials are in the Democratic Party and most have staked their career on being Democrats. In addition, the black community continues to vote Democratic in overwhelming numbers. For example, in the presidential elections since Lyndon Johnson in 1964, Democrats have won at least 85 percent of the black vote.

Black elected officials, the black community, and the nation as a whole must face soberly the racial, political, and economic challenges of the new century. America in the twenty-first century will be more multiracial than ever. The percent of Latinos and Asians will continue to grow, particularly on the East Coast, the West Coast, and in the Southwest. It will be in the interest of African Americans to seek common ground and coalitions with these communities.

The rise in racial animosity in the 1990s may signal a new era of intolerance that will require new approaches to America's age-old problem of race. Much of the battleground will be in the legislative arena, over everything from cuts in social spending to the elimination of civil rights programs, such as affirmative action. Black elected officials can be critical players in these contests, helping to draft progressive legislation and educating the public from their high-profile platform.

Perhaps the key challenge will be addressing the impact of the globalized economy as more and more jobs permanently disappear and the need for a highly-skilled labor force becomes more imperative. Black leaders must fight for inclusion of the black community in this new economic order. This will likely mean struggling to institute a broad program of intensive job training, the creation of public jobs, education in the new technologies, and efforts to retool black enterprises.

To win the coming battles, black elected officials and the black community must move beyond electoral politics as the principle vehicle for seeking benefits from the political system. No longer can elected officials remain largely unaccountable to the black community; they must be held to the same standard that all black leaders should be held to: commitment and sacrifice to the broad interests of the black community and to those who have been excluded, disenfranchised, and locked out of society. Those black elected officials who stand up to this standard will not only make a contribution in the best tradition of black leaders, but will also justify the immense investment that African Americans have made to put blacks in public office since first arriving on these shores.

APPENDIX

Black Presidential Candidates

In 1856, the Political Abolition Party nominated Gerrit Smith, who was white, for President and black abolitionist Frederick Douglas for Vice President.[1] In 1872, the Equal Rights Party nominated Victoria Claflin Woodhall for President and Frederick Douglass, once again, for Vice President. Douglass did not accept this nomination although his name did appear on the ballot in New York.[2]

In 1904, the Liberty Party nominated George Edwin Taylor of Ottumwa, Iowa, to be its Presidential candidate.[3] In a burst of candidate fervor, Taylor predicted very incorrectly that he could win 60 percent of black vote.

In the main, it has been radical political parties that have nominated blacks for President and Vice President. The Communist Party, for example, ran James Ford in 1932, 1936, and 1940 for Vice President.[4] In each campaign, he won nationally a little more than 2,000 votes.[5] Thirty-six years later, in 1968, the Communist Party nominated Charlene Mitchell as its Presidential candidate, the first black woman to be nominated to the position.[6]

Communist Party leader Jarvis Tyner ran for Vice President in 1972 and 1976, and activist and writer Angela Davis for Vice President in 1980 and 1984. In 1980, Davis won 45,023 votes on the ballot in 25 states and, in 1984, on the ballot in 30 states, she won 36,386 votes.[7]

In 1952, Charlotta Bass ran for Vice President on the Progressive Party ticket. Vincent Hallinen, a labor lawyer, was the presidential candidate. Bass owned and operated a black newspaper, *California Eagle*, in Los Angeles. The ticket won 140,023 votes in 27 states.[8] Hallinen and Bass were endorsed by the American Labor Party of New York, which, at the time, was running W. E. B. Du Bois for the U.S. Senate. Du Bois spoke at the party's national convention giving Hallinen and Bass a strong endorsement. She also had support of performer and activist Paul Robeson. Bass' campaign attacked President Eisenhow on the weakness and uselessness of his Fair Employment Practices Commission (FEPC). She stated, "The states have done with FEPC the same thing they have done about lynching, terror, and discrimination in housing, the same thing the Truman administration has done about the very heart and soul of the Negro people's problems: *nothing*.[9]"

In 1960, the Alabama-based nationalist Afro-American Party nominated all black candidates, including Rev. Clennon King for President and Reginald Carter for Vice President. They received 1,485 votes. In 1968, Black Panther leader Eldridge Cleaver won 195,135 votes on the ballot in 19 states on the Peace and Freedom Party ticket.[10] In that same year, on the similarly-named Freedom and Peace Party, black comedian and social activist Dick Gregory won 148,622 votes as that party's nominee.[11] The Socialist Workers Party nominated Paul Boutelle, an African-American, to be their presidential candidate in 1968.

In the 1970s, black candidates for President and Vice President emerged. In 1972, Rep. Shirley Chisholm (D-NY), ran for the Democratic Party nomination for President. She won 430,703 votes in 14 states.[12] In 1976, two black women ran for the highest offices in the land: Margaret Wright and Willie Mae Reid. Wright ran for President on the People's Party ticket. She won 49,024 votes in 6 states. Reid, on the Socialist Workers Party ticket, ran for Vice President winning 91,314 votes in 28 states.[13] She ran again in 1992, also as the Vice Presidential nominee, winning only won 23,096 in 12 states.[14]

At the 1968 Democratic National Convention, Rev. Channing Phillips won 46.5 presidential votes from 17 state delegations and 21 of the 23 votes available from the District of Columbia for total of 67.5 votes.[15] At the same convention, Georgia state representative and civil rights activist Julian Bond won 87.5 votes for Vice President (although he was actually legally too young at the time to be Vice President).[16] Bond supported the tactic by arguing that it would be "a technique to win more say-so in the political convention."[17]

Although there is no record of the Republican Party ever nominating a black for either President or Vice President, some black Republicans have stated that they believe that they could have achieved some measure of success as a candidate. For example, in 1971, Republican Arthur Fletcher, former Assistant Secretary of Labor, United Nations delegation member, and executive director of the United Negro College Fund, said, "I believe I could have gone to the Republican convention with 600–800 votes on the first ballot for Vice President."[18]

The black community has shown support for such campaigns. In August 1971, *Jet* magazine found that 98 percent of their readers felt a black man should run for President in 1972.[19] Ninety-three percent of those surveyed felt then that the candidate should be Julian Bond. Other black leaders that were mentioned included Cleveland mayor Carl Stokes, Rep. John Conyers, Sen. Edward Brooke, and Shirley Chisholm, who only received 5 percent of *Jet* readers' support.[20]

SOURCE NOTES

CHAPTER 1

1. Lerone Bennett Jr., *Before the Mayflower: A History of Black America* (New York: Penguin Books, 1993), p. 458.
2 Ibid., p. 458.
3 Ibid., p. 461.
4 Bruce A. Ragsdale and Joel D. Treese, *Black Americans in Congress, 1870–1989* (Washington, D.C.: U.S. Government Printing Office, 1990), p. 74; and Robert Allen, *Reluctant Reformers: Racism and Social Reform Movements in the United States* (Washington, D.C.: Howard University Press, 1983), p. 43.
5 John Hope Franklin, *From Freedom to Slavery: A History of Negro Americans* (New York: Vintage, 1969), p. 162.
6 Sonia Jarvis, "Historical Overview: African Americans and the Evolution of Voting Rights," in Ralph C. Gomes and Linda Faye Williams, *From Exclusion to Inclusion: The Long Struggle for African American Political Power* (New York: Greenwood Press, 1992), p. 18.

7. Franklin, pp. 128–129.

8. "He has waged a cruel war against human nature itself, violating its most sacred rights of life and liberty in the persons of a distant people who never offended him, captivating and carrying them into slavery in another hemisphere, or to incur miserable death in their transportation thither. This piratical warfare, the opprobirum of *infidel* powers, is the warfare of the *Christian* king of Great Britain. Determined to keep open a market where men should be bought and sold, he prostituted his negative for suppressing every legislative attempt to prohibit or to restrain this excrable commerce. And that this assemblage of horrors might want no fact of distinguished die, he is now exciting those very people to rise in the arms among us, and to purchase that liberty of which he has deprived them, by murdering the people on whom he also obtruded them." [emphasis in the original] See Albert P. Blaustein and Robert L. Zangrando, *Civil Rights and African Americans: A Documentary History* (Evanston, IL: Northwestern University Press, 1991), pp. 43–44.

9. Livermore, p. 55.

10. Ibid., p. 71.

11. Kevin Coleman and Daryl Harris, *Black Electoral Patricipation and Representation* (Washington, D.C.: Congressional Research Service, the Library of Congress, 1993), p. 4.

12. Jarvis, p. 22.

13. Ibid., p. 40.

14. Blaustein and Zangrando, p. 149.

15. Lincoln stated in a letter in 1862, "My Paramount objective is to save the Union, and not either to save or destroy slavery." Blaustein and Zangrando, pp. 195–196.

CHAPTER 2

1. Lerone Bennett, *Black Power, U.S.A.: The Human Side of Reconstruction* (Chicago: Johnson Publishing Co., 1967), p. 52.
2. Eric Foner, "African Americans in Public Office During the Era of Reconstruction: A Profile," *Reconstruction*, Vol. 2., No. 2, 1993, p. 20.
3. James Ridgeway, *Blood in the Face: The Ku Klux Klan, Aryan Nations, Nazi Skinheads, and the Rise of a New White Culture* (New York: Thunder's Mouth Press, 1990), p. 33.
4. Foner, p. 25.
5. W. E. B. Du Bois, *Black Reconstruction in America* (New York: Atheneum, 1979), p. 391.
6. Peter Camejo, *Racism, Revolution, Reaction, 1861–1877: The Rise and Fall of Radical Reconstruction* (New York: Monad Press, 1976), p. 164.
7. Bruce A. Ragsdale and Joel D. Treese, *Black Americans in Congress, 1870–1989* (Washington, D.C.: U.S. Government Printing Office, 1990), p. 124.
8. Ibid., Bennett, *Black Power, U.S.A.*, p. 133.
9. Ibid., p. 59.
10. Ibid., p. 6.
11. Ibid., p. 74.
12. Ibid., pp. 74–75.
13. Ibid., p. 69.
14. Ibid., p. 80.
15. Ibid., p. 84.
16. Ibid., p. 85.
17. Ibid., p. 82.
18. Ibid., p. 99.
19. Ibid., p. 76.
20. Ragsdale Treese, pp. 7–9.
21. Ibid., p. 22.
22. Excerpted from *Congressional Record*, 56th Congress,

2nd Session, January 29, 1901, pp. 1636–1638. Ibid.,
pp. 379-80.

23. Angela Davis, *Women, Race & Class* (New York: Vintage Books, 1983), p. 112.
24. Chandler Davidson, "Black Voter Dilution: An Overview," in Chandler Davidson, ed., *Minority Voter Dilution* (Washington, D.C.: Howard University Press, 1989), pp. 1–23.
25. J. Morgan Kousser, "The Undermining of the First Reconstruction: Lessons for the Second," in Chandler Davidson, ed., *Minority Voter Dilution* (Washington, D.C.: Howard University Press, 1989), p. 34.
26. By keeping millions of potential voters out of the process, the small elite in office could maintain their positions of power. Stetson Kennedy, *Jim Crow Guide: The Way It Was* (Boca Raton, FL: Florida Atlantic University Press, 1990), p. 150.
27. Marcus D. Pohlmann, *Black Politics in Conservative America* (New York: Longman, 1990), p. 114.
28. Richard Pollenberg, *One Nation Divisible: Class, Race, and Ethnicity in the United States Since 1938* (New York: Penguin Books, 1980), p. 159.
29. Kennedy, p. 156.
30. Henry Lee Moon, *Balance of Power: The Negro Vote* (Garden City, NY: Doubleday and Company, Inc., 1948), p. 245.
31. Ibid., p. 246.
32. Kennedy, p. 152.
33. Paul Lewinson, *Race, Class, and Party: A History of Negro Suffrage and White Politics in the South* (New York: Grosset & Dunlap, 1965), p. 81.
34. Kennedy, p. 150.

CHAPTER 3

1. Kaye M. Teall, *Notes from Black History in Oklahoma* (Oklahoma City: Oklahoma City Schools, 1971), p. 156.

2. Ibid., p. 154.
3. Ibid., p. 154.
4. Ibid., p. 167.
5. Ibid., p. 173.
6. Ibid., p. 177.
7. Norman L. Crockett, *The Black Towns* (Lawrence, KS: The Regents of Kansas, 1979), pp. 81–82.
8. Ibid., p. 110.
9. Ibid., p. 111.
10. Ibid., p. 113.
11. Ibid., p. 92.
12. Ibid., p. 95.
13. Ibid., p. 96.
14. Ibid., p. 97.
15. Ibid., p. 109.

CHAPTER 4

1. Chuck Stone, *Black Political Power* (New York: Delta Books, 1970), p. 39.
2. Ibid., Moon, pp. 18–19.
3. David Bositis, *Blacks and the 1992 Democratic National Convention* (Washington, D.C.: Joint Center for Political and Economic Studies, 1992), p. 29.
4. Ibid., Moon, p. 31.
5. Lenneal J. Henderson, Jr., "Black Politics and American Presidential Elections," in Michael B. Preston, Lenneal J. Henderson, Jr., and Paul L. Puryear, *The New Black Politics: The Search for Political Power* (New York: Longman, Inc., 1987), p. 8.
6. Ibid., Moon, p. 10.
7. Jack M. Bloom, *Class, Race & the Civil Rights Movement* (Bloomington, IN: Indiana University Press, 1987), p. 76.
8. Bloom, p. 80.
9. Ibid., p. 80.
10. Manning Marable, *Race, Reform and Rebellion: The Second Reconstruction in Black America, 1945–1982,* (Jack-

son, MS: University Press on Mississippi, 1984), pp. 24–27.

11. Bloom, p. 82.
12. Bloom, p. 81.
13. Benjamin J. Wallace, "The Negro People's Liberation Movement," *Political Affairs*, September 1948, pp. 880–98.
14. Bloom, p. 84.
15. Rick Hampson, "Private Letters Reveal Truman's Racist Attitudes," *Washington Times*, October 25, 1991.
16. Ibid., p. A1.
17. Edward T. Clayton, *The Negro Politician: His Success and Failure* (Chicago: Johnson Publishing Co., 1964), p. 164.
18. Ibid., p. 92.
19. Ibid., p. 93.
20. Ibid., Marable, p. 27.
21. Stetson Kennedy, *Jim Crow Guide: The Way It Was* (Boca Raton, FL: Florida Atlantic University Press, 1990), p. 153.
22. Clayton, pp. 62–63.
23. Stone, pp. 57–59.
24. W. E. B. Du Bois, *In Battle For Peace: The Story of My 83rd Birthday* (New York: Masses and Mainstream Press, 1952), p. 44.
25. Ibid., p. 50.
26. Ibid., Marable, p. 28.
27. Ibid., Clayton, pp. 158–159.

CHAPTER 5

1. Manning Marable, *Race, Reform and Rebellion: The Second Reconstruction in Black America, 1945–1982* (Jackson, MS: University Press of Mississippi, 1984), p. 10.
2. Stewart E. Tolnay and E. M. Beck, "Rethinking the

Role of Racial Violence in the Great Migration," Alferdteen Harrison, ed., *Black Exodus: The Great Migration From the American South* (Jackson, MS: University Press of Mississippi, 1991), pp. 27, 33.

3. Ibid., Tolnay and Beck, p. 20.

4. Carole Marks, "The Social and Economic Life of the Southern Blacks During Migration," Alferdteen Harrison, ed., *Black Exodus: The Great Migration From the American South* (Jackson, MS: University Press of Mississippi), 1991), p. 46.

5, Ibid., Marable, p. 9.

6. Harold Baron, *The Demand for Black Labor: Historic Notes on the Political Economy of Racism* (Somerville, MA: New England Free Press, 1971), p. 20. Also see Melvin M. Leiman, *The Political Economy of Racism: A History* (Boulder, CO: Pluto Press, 1993).

7. Ibid., Clayton, p. 54.

8. Stetson Kennedy, *Jim Crow Guide: The Way It Was* (Boca Raton, FL: Florida Atlantic University Press, 1990), p. 54.

9. Ibid., Marable, p. 22.

10. Philip S. Foner, *Organized Labor and the Black Worker, 1619–1973* (New York: International Publishers, 1974), p. 280.

11. Charles V. Hamilton, *Adam Clayton Powell: The Political Biography of an American Dilemma* (New York: Collier Books, 1991), p. 315.

12. Hamilton, pp. 434–444.

13. Ibid., Clayton, p. 87.

CHAPTER 6

1. See Clayborn Carson, *In Struggle: SNCC and the Black Awakening of the 1960s* (Cambridge, MA: Harvard University Press, 1981).

2. See Kay Mills, *This Little Light of Mine: The Life of Fannie Lou Hamer* (New York: Dutton, 1993).
3. Sean Dennis Cashman, *African Americans and the Quest for Civil Rights, 1900–1990* (New York: Plumb, 1989), p. 189.
4. Charles E. Fager, *Selma 1965: The March That Changed the South* (Boston: Beacon Press, 1985), p. 57.
5. Ibid., p. 58.
6. Manning Marable, *Race, Reform and Rebellion: The Second Reconstruction in Black America, 1945–1982* (Jackson: University Press of Mississippi, 1984), p. 88.
7. Lerone Bennett Jr., *Before the Mayflower: A History of Black America* (New York: Penguin Books, 1988), p 416.
8. Robert Weisbolt, *Freedom Bound: A History of America's Civil Rights Movement* (New York: Plumb, 1991), p. 149.
9. John Hope Franklin, *From Slavery to Freedom: A History of Negro Americans* (New York: Vintage Books, 1967), p. 638.
10. Steven F. Lawson, *Black Ballots: Voting Rights in the South, 1944–1969* (New York: Columbia University Press, 1976), p. 318.
11. Ibid.
12. Ibid., p. 321.
13. Ibid., Weisbrot, p. 152.
14. Ibid., Lawson, p. 329.
15. Marcus D. Pohlmann, *Black Politics in Conservative America* (New York: Longman, 1990), p. 141.
16. Ibid., p. 12.
17. Robert C. Smith, "The Changing Shape of Urban Black Politics: 1960–1970," *Annals,* September 1978, pp. 16–28.
18. Ibid., p. 21.
19. Ibid., p. 68.

CHAPTER 7

1. William L. Clay, *Just Permanent Interests: Black Americans in Congress 1870–1991* (New York: Amistad, 1992), p. 165.
2. Clay, p. 117.
3. Clay, pp. 146–147.
4. Ronald W. Waters, *Black Presidential Politics: A Strategic Approach* (Albany, NY: State University of New York, 1988), p. 92.
5. Ibid., p. 89.
6. Clay, p. 209.
7. Clay, p. 209.
8. Clay, p. 229.
9. Ibid., p. 232.
10. Ibid., p. 232.
11. Manning Marable, *Black American Politics: From Washington Marches to Jesse Jackson* (London: Version, 1985), p. 180.
12. "Klan Holds White Voter Registration Drives, Backs Candidates," *Klanwatch Intelligence Report,* July 1984, p. 4.
13. *It's Time to Reinvest in America* (Washington, D.C.: The Campaign for New Priorities, 1992), p. 4.
14. see Marable.
15. Ibid.
16. Salim Muwakkil, "Follow the Leader?", *In These Times,* February 22, 1993, p. 29.
17. Ibid.
18. Kent Jenkins, Jr., "Mfume on the Move," *Washington Post,* December 8, 1992.
19. Preceding Braun were Hiram R. Revels (R-MS), 1870–1871; Blanche K. Bruce (R-MS), 1875–1881; and Edward W. Brooke (R-MS), 1966–1978. During

his two terms in the Senate, Brooke did not become a member of the Congressional Black Caucus.

20. At the beginning of the 103rd, the House leadership agreed to give the delegates the right to vote on the floor except on final passage of a bill. This was viewed initially as an advance because most controversies on legislation are settled before the final passage. The House leadership added a provision, however, that explicitly stated that if the delegates' votes made the difference on any particular vote, then that vote would be taken over again without the delegates participating. This rule effectively nullified the delegates' votes.

21. Bositis, p. 35.

22. Juan Williams, "From Caucus to Coalition," *Washington Post,* January 10, 1993, p. C2.

CHAPTER 8

1. Sheila D. Collins, *The Rainbow Challenge: The Jackson Campaign and the Future of U.S. Politics* (New York: Monthly Review Press, 1986), p. 114.

2. Manning Marable, *Black American Politics: From the Washington Marches to Jesse Jackson* (London: Verso, 1985), p. 223.

3. Vernon Jarrett, "Evidence of Pre-Election Racism," *Chicago Tribune,* February 18, 1983.

4. Mike Royko, "Racist Finale: An Odorous Byrne Ploy," *Chicago Sun-Times,* February 22, 1983.

5. Ibid., Marable, *Black American Politics,* p. 230.

6. Ibid., p. 233.

7. Ibid., p. 233.

8. Ibid., p. 237.

9. Ibid., p. 237.

10. Walters, p. 115.

11. Ibid., p. 120.

12. Paulette Pierce, "The Roots of the Rainbow Coalition," *The Black Scholar,* March/April 1988, p. 9.
13. Thomas E. Cavanagh and Lorn S. Foster, *Jesse Jackson's Campaigns: The Primaries and Caucuses* (Washington, D.C.: Joint Center for Political Studies, 1984), p 2.
14. Ibid., p. 4.
15. Ibid., p. 5.
16. Marable, p. 119.
17. *Toward a Just Society and a Peaceful World,* p. 6.
18. Ibid., p. 8.
19. Ibid., pp. 13–14.
20. Walters, p. 172.
21. Clarence Lusane, "Jesse Jackson's Quest for the Presidency: Seizing the Historic Moment," *Critical Social Issues,* Spring 1990, p. 9.
22. "Election Totals in Presidential Race," *Black Political Agenda '92,* November/December 20, 1991, p. 1.
23. Larry A. Still, "Dr. Fulani Leads Presidential Race," *National Chronicle,* December 20, 1991, p. 14.
24. Ibid., p. 14.

CHAPTER 9

1. Michael Lind, "The Southern Coup," *The New Republic,* June 19, 1995, p. 23.
2. See Clarence Lusane, *Pipe Dream Blues: Racism and the War on Drugs* (Boston: South End Press, 1991).
3. *It's Time to Reinvest in America* (Washington, D.C.: The Campaign for New Priorities, 1992), p. 4.
4. Ibid., p. 8.
5. William M. Welch, "Southern Lights Are Now Shining on Republicans," *USA Today,* November 10, 1994.
6. "Election Analysis," *The New York Times,* November 10, 1994.

7. Donald L. Barlette and James B. Steele, *America, What Went Wrong?* (Kansas City: Andrews and McNeel, 1992), p. 8.
8. National Urban League, *State of Black America 1993* (New York: National Urban League, 1993), p. 168.
9. "Number of Americans in Poverty up for Fourth Year," press release, Department of Commerce, Census Bureau, October 6, 1994.
10. Rochelle Sharpe, "In Latest Recession, Only Blacks Suffered Net Employment Loss," *Wall Street Journal,* September 14, 1993.
11. Harriet A. Washington, "Examining Health Care Reform," *Emerge,* December/January 1994, p. 35.
12. Mike Snider, "Blacks' Medical Care Often Lacking," *USA Today,* July 20, 1993.
13. Ibid.
14. Mary Jordan, "Local Child Abuse and Neglect Cases Reach a Record Number," *Washington Post,* December 18, 1992.
15. Chris Booker, "Racism: Challenges and Changes for the 1990s," unpublished report, 1992, p. 8.
16. Ibid., p. 8.
17. Ibid., pp. 7–8.
18. Isabel Wilkerson and Angela Mitchell, "Staying Alive! The Challenge of Improving Black America's Health," *Emerge,* September 1991, p. 28.
19. Manning Marable, "In Critical Condition: Black Health Care and the 1992 Election," *Black Political Agenda '92,* September 1992, p. 7.
20. Gerard Bushell and Jocelyn Sargent, "Racing for the Top: Race and the 1993 New York City Mayoral Election," unpublished paper, September, 1994, p. 8.
21. Ibid., p. 8.
22. Guy E. De Weever, "'I Know It When I See It': Supreme Court Attacks Voting Rights," *Black Political Agenda,* First Quarter 1995, p. 4.

APPENDIX

1. Hanes Walton, Jr. and Ronald Clark, "Black Presidential Candidates Past and Present," *New South: A Quarterly Review of Southern Affairs,* Spring 1972, p. 16.
2. Ibid., p. 17.
3. Ibid., p. 17.
4. Ibid., p. 18.
5. Ibid., p. 19.
6. Ibid., p. 19.
7. Hanes Walton, Jr. ed., *Black Politics and Black Political Behavior: A Linkage Analysis* (Westport, CT: Praeger, 1995), p. 267.
8. Ibid., p. 267.
9. Ibid., p. 258.
10. Hanes and Clark, p. 19.
11. Ibid., p. 19.
12. Walton, p. 267.
13. Ibid., p. 267.
14. Ibid., p. 267.
15. Walton and Clark, p. 20.
16. Ibid., p. 20.
17. Ibid, p. 15.
18. Ibid, p. 16.
19. Ronald W. Walters, *Black Presidential Politics in America: A Strategic Approach* (Albany, NY: State University of New York Press, 1988), p. 115.
20. Walton and Clark, p. 15.

INDEX

Abernathy, Rev. David, 87
Adams, Abigail, 12
Adams, John, 12
African Institute, 17
African Methodist Episcopal
    (AME) church, 16
Afro-American Colonializa-
    tion Company, 33
Afro-American Party, 138
Allen, Richard, 15, 16
American Colonialization
    Society, 17
American Labor Party, 48, 138
American Nazi Party, 115
Attucks, Crispus, 12

Back-to-Africa movement, 17
    see also Repatriation,
    Africa
Baraka, Imamu Amiri, 61, 83,
    86

Baron, Harold, 52
Barry, Marion, 128, 131–132
Bass, Charlotta, 138
Berry, Mary Frances, 109
Berry, Theodore, 47
Bevel, James, 115–116
Bilbo, Theodore, 46
Black Panthers, 81, 138
Blyden, Edward 15, 17
Bond, Julian, 86, 139, 140
Booker, Chris, 127
Bork, Robert, 88, 113
Boutelle, Paul, 138
Braun, Carol Mosely, 94
Brimmer, Andrew, 79
Brooke, Edward, 77, 79, 82, 140
Brown, John, 19
Brown, Willie, 86
Bruce, Blanche Kelson, 24, 25
Bush, George, 90, 115,
    120–121, 126

Bushell, Gerard, 130
Byrne, Jane, 101, 103, 105

Campbell, Ben, 121
Cardozo, Francis, 24
Carmichael, Stokely, 77
Carter, Jimmy, 86
Carter, Reginald, 138
Chisolm, Shirley, 80, 84, 86,
    139, 140
Citizens Party, 36
Civil Rights Act (1957), 61
Civil Rights Act (1964), 63
Civil Rights Bill (1991), 90
Clark, James, Jr., 70, 71, 72
Clay, William, 82
Cleaver, Eldridge, 138
Clewis, Richard, 105
Clinton, Bill, 93, 115, 118, 119
Coleman, Marshall, 131
Colored Immigration Bureau,
    33
Communist Party, 137–138
Congressional Black Caucus,
    61, 80, 81–99, 108, 134
Congress of Racial Equality
    (CORE), 66
Conyers, John, 61, 64–65, 83,
    86, 88, 94, 140
Council of Federated Organi-
    zations, 66
Crockett, Norman, 37
Crummell, Alexander, 15, 17
Cuffee, Paul, 15, 17
Currin, Green I., 35

Daley, Richard, 103
Daley, Richard, Jr., 103
Daniels, Ron, 115

Darrow, Clarence, 54
Davis, Angela, 138
Davis, Benjamin, 44, 47
Dawson, William, 47, 55
Delaney, Martin, 15, 17
Dellums, Ron, 84, 86, 88, 94,
    134
Democratic Congressional
    Campaign Committee
    (DCCC), 95, 97
Democratic Leadership Coun-
    cil (DLC), 118–119
Democratic Party, 18, 25–28,
    34, 36, 39–44, 46, 49–51,
    54–55, 58, 68–69, 73–74,
    82–84, 86–88, 9396, 100,
    103, 105, 107, 108, 112–
    115, 118–120, 121, 122,
    124, 125, 128, 131, 132,
    135, 139
Democratic Select Committee
    (DSC), 81–82
DePriest, Oscar, 52, 54
Dewey, Thomas, 42–44
Diggs, Charles, Jr., 46, 61–62,
    81, 83, 86
Dinkins, David, 128, 130–131
Dirksen, Everett, 73
Douglass, Frederick, 19, 137
Du Bois, W.E.B., 44, 48, 138

Eastland, James, 73
Eisenhower, Dwight, 46, 58, 138
Elected officials
    prior to Civil War, 11, 17,
        137
    during Reconstruction,
        20, 21, 24, 25, 26, 27,
        28, 29, 137

late 19th century, 29, 33, 34, 35, 36, 40
20th century, 31, 35, 36, 42, 43, 44, 46, 47, 48, 50–65, 75, 77, 79, 80, 81, 84, 93–99, 100–116, 117–125, 128–136
Elliott, Robert Brown, 24
Epton, Bernard, 105
Equal Rights Party, 137
Ervin, Sam, 73
Espy, Mike, 119

Fauntroy, Walter, 83, 86
Federalist Party, 18
Fields, Cleo, 113
First Grand Independent Brotherhood (FGIB), 33
Fletcher, Arthur, 139
Flynn, Raymond, 101
Ford, Gerald, 86
Ford, Henry, 51
Ford, James, 137
Franks, Gary, 94, 122, 134
Frazer, Vincent, 94
Free African Society, 16
Freedom and Peace Party, 138
Fulani, Lenora, 115

Garnet, Henry H., 15
Gephardt, Richard, 118
Gibbs, Jonathan C., 24
Gingrich, Newt, 93
Giuliani, Rudolph, 131
Goldwater, Barry, 69, 120
Gore, Al, 118, 119
Grant, Ulysses S., 22
Gray, Bill, 88, 119

Gregory, Dick, 138
Guinn v. United States, 30

Hall, Prince, 15
Hallinen, Vincent, 138
Hamer, Fannie Lou, 66, 68, 69, 113
Harper v. Virginia Board of Elections, 30
Harris, Patricia, 79, 86
Harrison, William, 34
Hasting, Alcee, 92
Hatcher, Richard, 61, 83, 86
Hawkins, Augustus, 61, 63–64
Hayes, Rutherford B., 28
Henry, Patrick 13
Hillard, Earl, 95
Holman, Carl, 110
Hooks, Benjamin, 108, 109
Hoover, Herbert, 54
House Un-American Activities Committee (HUAC), 58, 65
Humphrey, Hubert, 69

International Emigration Association, 17

Jack, Hulan, 48
Jackson, Jesse, 86, 100, 101, 103, 107–115, 119, 120, 128
Jackson, Jimmy Lee, 70, 71
Jackson, Maynard, 86
Jacobs, John, 108
James, Esther, 58, 60
Jefferson, Bill, 97
Jefferson, Thomas, 13, 15

Jim Crow laws, 35, 38, 50, 55
Johnson, Lyndon, 68–69,
    72–75, 79, 135
Joint Center for Political and
    Economic Studies, 82
Jones, Elaine, 134
Jordan, Barbara, 75, 80

Kelly, Edmund, 105
Kelly, Sharon Pratt, 132
Kennedy, John F., 49
Kennedy, Robert, 74
Kennedy, Ted, 86, 103
Keyes, Alan, 122
King, Clennon, 138
King, Coretta Scott, 49, 71, 109
King, Dr. Martin Luther, Jr.,
    49, 65, 68–74, 79, 81, 88,
    108, 109, 116
King, Martin Luther, Sr., 49
King, Mel, 101
Knights of the White Camel-
    lia, 21
Kousser, J. Morgan, 29
Ku Klux Klan, 21, 23, 87, 115

Labor Party, 124
Langston, John Mercer, 11
Larouche, Lyndon, 115–116
Laurino, Anthony, 105
Leisdesdorf, William, 11
Leland, Mickey, 92
Lewis, John, 95, 97
Liberty Party, 11, 137
Limbaugh, Rush, 122
Lincoln, Abraham, 18, 75
Louis, Joe, 44, 31, 33, 50,
    113, 114, 134
Lowery, Joseph, 109

Loyal Leagues, 23

Majerczyk, Aloysisu, 105
Malcolm X, 70–71
Marcantonio, Vito, 48, 58
Marshall, Thurgood, 79
Martin, Luther, 13
Marzullo, Vito, 105
Maybank, Burnet R., 31
McCabe, Edwin P., 32, 34
McCulloch, William, 74
McDowell, Calvin, 33
McGovern, George, 86
McKinney, Cynthia, 95,
    97
Melchoir, George, 39
Mfume, Kweisi, 90, 92, 97
Migration movement, north-
    ern 50, 51, 52, 79
Migration movement,
    western, *see* Western
    settlement
Miller v. Johnson, 134
Mississippi Freedom Democ-
    ratic Party (MFDP), 68,
    69
Mitchell, Arthur, 54, 55
Mitchell, Charlene, 137
Mitchell, Clarence III, 86
Mitchell, Parren, 86
Mitchell v. United States et al.,
    55
Mondale, Walter, 103, 109,
    112
Montgomery, Isaiah T., 39
Moon, Henry Lee, 42
Moses, Robert, 66, 68
Moss, Tom, 33
Nash, William Beverly, 21

National Association for the
Advancement of Colored
People (NAACP), 43, 66,
83, 108, 109, 134
National Black Caucus of
Local Elected Officials, 80
National Black Caucus of
State Legislatures, 80
National Black Independent
Political Party, 115
National Black Political
Assembly, 83, 107, 115
National Black Women's
Political Leadership
Caucus, 80
National Committee for Independent Political Action,
124
National Conference of Black
Mayors, 80
National Equal Rights
League. *See* National
Negro Convention
(NNC) movement
Nationalism, black
prior to Civil War, 15
after Civil War, 32
20th century, 77, 83, 84,
138
National Negro Convention
(NNC) movement, 17
National Urban League, 108,
126
Nation of Islam, 70
Nelson, Laura, 39
New Alliance Party, 115
Nix, Robert, Sr., 61, 62
Nixon, Richard, 49, 82, 86,
120

North
and slavery, 13, 18;
and voting, 15, 25, 29, 42,
50, 54
Norton, Eleanor Holmes, 94,
97

Oklahoma Immigration Association, 33
Operation PUSH, 101, 108

Pale Faces, 21
Patterson, Basil, 86
Payne, Donald, 92
Peace and Freedom Party,
138
People's Party, 36, 139
Perez, Leander, 73
Perot, H. Ross, 114, 124
Philips, Channing, 139
Pierce, Sam, 88
Plessy v. Ferguson, 29
Political Abolition Party, 137
Populist Party, 36
Powell, Adam Clayton, Jr., 46,
47, 57–61, 62
Price, Sterling, 23
Progressive Party, 43, 44,
138

Rainey, Joseph Hayne, 25
Rangel, Charles, 60, 86
Ransier, Alonzo Jacob, 22
Ray, John, 132
Reagan, Ronald, 65, 87, 88,
90, 100, 101, 108, 113,
115, 120–122, 126, 127
Reconstruction era, 20, 24,
27–28, 32, 117

Red Shirts, 21
Reeb, James, 70
Reid, Willie Mae, 139
Repatriation, Africa, 17, 19
Republican Party, 18, 22, 24,
    25, 27, 28, 29, 34, 35, 36,
    39, 40, 41, 43, 46, 49, 51,
    54, 55, 58, 69, 73, 74, 77,
    82, 83, 92, 93, 94, 95, 100,
    105, 108, 114, 118, 119,
    120–122, 124, 125, 131,
    135, 139
Revels, Hiram, 24, 25
Revolutionary Action Move-
    ment, 81
Reynolds, Mel, 97
Ricks, Willie, 77
Rittenberg, Ivan, 105
Robeson, Paul, 44, 138
Roosevelt, Franklin Delano,
    42, 55
Rush, Bobby, 95
Russell, S. Douglas, 40
Rustin, Bayard, 83

Sargent, Jocelyn, 130
Scott, Dred, decision, 19
Selma (Alabama) march
    (1965),70–73
76 Association, 21
Shaw v. Reno, 133
Shelby, Richard, 121
Singleton, Benjamin, 32
Slavery
    and Civil War, 19
    as issue in colonial times,
        12
    as issue with political par-
        ties, 18

results of after Civil War,
    20
Smith v. Allwright, 31
Smith, Gerrit, 137
Smith, Howard, 74
Smith, Robert, 77
Socialist Workers Party, 138,
    139
South
    and slavery, 13, 18
    and state constitutional
        conventions, 23, 26, 29,
        30, 39
    and voting, 15, 21, 23,
        26–31, 35, 43, 46–47,
        49–50, 66, 68, 74–75,
        95, 113, 114, 120–121
    conditions after Civil
        War, 21, 32
Southern Christian Leader-
    ship Conference (SCLC),
    66, 70, 109, 116
States' Rights Party, 43
Stewart, Will, 33
Stokes, Carl, 140
Stokes, Louis, 82, 86
Student Non-Violent Coor-
    dinating Committee
    (SNCC), 66, 70, 72, 77
Supreme Court (U.S.), 19,
    29, 30, 31, 55, 60, 79, 88,
    90, 113, 121, 122, 133–
    134
Sutton, Percy, 86

Taney, Roger B., 19
Taylor, George Edwin, 137
The New Party (TNP), 124
Thomas, Clarence, 90, 122

Thomas, Mabel, 113
Thurmond, Strom, 43
Tilden, Samuel J., 28
Tolson, Arthur, 33
Truman, Bess, 44
Truman, Harry, 43, 44, 46, 58, 138
Turner, Henry McNeal, 15, 17
Twilight, Alexander Lucius, 11
Tyner, Jarvis, 138

Voting
   prior to Revolutionary War, 12
   after Revolutionary War, 15
   prior to Civil War, 15, 18, 19;
   during Reconstruction, 20–24, 26, 27
   late 19th century, 29, 30, 31
   20th century, 35, 36, 40, 41 44, 46, 48–49, 66, 68, 70, 75, 86, 101, 103, 105, 112-116, 118–125, 128–136, 137–140
   restrictions, 12, 15, 29, 30, 31, 33, 36, 38, 39, 46, 49, 55, 57, 66, 68, 70, 72, 74, 83
Voting Rights Act (1965), 31, 49, 65, 65–77, 80, 87, 133
Vrdolyak, Edward, 103, 107

Wallace, George, 71
Wallace, Henry A., 43, 44
Washington, Booker T., 37, 40
Washington, Craig, 90, 92, 97
Washington, George, 13
Washington, Harold, 101, 103, 105, 107
Waters, Maxine, 97
Watt, Melvin, 134
Watts, J. C., 94, 122, 134
Weaver, Robert C., 79
Western settlement, 32, 40
Whig Party, 18
White Brotherhood, 21
White, George, 28
White, Walter, 43
Wilder, Douglas, 119, 128, 131
Wilkins, Roy, 83
Wilkinson, Bill, 87
Williams, Armstrong, 122
Williams, Edward Bennett, 58
Williams, Hosea, 87
Woodhull, Victoria, 137
Wright, Margaret, 139

Young, Andrew, 75, 86, 108
Young, Coleman, 108
Young, Whitney, Jr., 83